YORK NOTES

# The Merchant of Venice

## William Shakespeare

Notes by Michael and Mary Alexander

 Longman  York Press

Exterior picture of the Globe Theatre reproduce by permission of the
Raymond Mander and Joe Mitchenson Theatre Collection
Reconstruction of the Globe Theatre interior reprinted from Hodges:
**The Globe Restored** (1968) by permission of Oxford University Press

YORK PRESS
322 Old Brompton Road, London SW5 9JH

PEARSON EDUCATION LIMITED
Edinburgh Gate, Harlow,
Essex CM20 2JE, United Kingdom
Associated companies, branches and representatives throughout the world

First published 1998
Eighth impression 2003

ISBN 0-582-32924-8

Designed by Vicki Pacey, Trojan Horse, London
Phototypeset by Gem Graphics, Trenance, Mawgan Porth, Cornwall
Colour reproduction and film output by Spectrum Colour
Produced by Pearson Education Asia Limited, Hong Kong

# CONTENTS

PART ONE

| INTRODUCTION | How to Study a Play | 5 |
| | Reading *The Merchant of Venice* | 6 |

PART TWO

| SUMMARIES | Note on the Text | 8 |
| | Synopsis | 9 |
| | Detailed Summaries | |
| | Act I | 10 |
| | Act II | 16 |
| | Act III | 24 |
| | Act IV | 31 |
| | Act V | 36 |

PART THREE

CRITICAL APPROACHES

| | Comedy and Convention | 40 |
| | Themes | 41 |
| | Love, Marriage and Friendship | 41 |
| | Money | 42 |
| | Justice and Mercy | 44 |
| | Characterisation | 45 |
| | Antonio | 45 |
| | Bassanio | 47 |
| | Portia | 47 |
| | Shylock | 48 |
| | Minor Characters | 49 |
| | Style and Language | 50 |
| | Verse Drama: Prose and Poetry | 50 |
| | Language, Imagery and Theme | 51 |

PART FOUR

TEXTUAL ANALYSIS
 Text 1: Introducing Shylock    55
 Text 2: The Trial's Conclusion   58
 Text 3: Lorenzo and Jessica: A Duet 61

PART FIVE

BACKGROUND Shakespeare's Life     66
  His Dramatic Career    67
  The Texts of Shakespeare's Plays 68
 Shakespeare and the English Renaissance 70
 Shakespeare's Theatre    73
  Reading Shakespeare   78
 Literary Background    81
  Sources      81
 Historical Background    83
  Jews and Christians   83
  Usury      84
  Anti-Semitism    84
  Venice      85

PART SIX

CRITICAL HISTORY
 Bibliography     87
 Stage History     87
 Critical Reception    89

PART SEVEN

BROADER PERSPECTIVES
 Further Reading    92
 Chronology     94
Literary Terms      96
Authors of this Note    97

# PART ONE

# INTRODUCTION

## HOW TO STUDY A PLAY

Studying on your own requires self-discipline and a carefully thought-out work plan in order to be effective.

- Drama is a special kind of writing (the technical term is 'genre') because it needs a performance in the theatre to arrive at a full interpretation of its meaning. Try to imagine that you are a member of the audience when reading the play. Think about how it could be presented on the stage, not just about the words on the page.

- Drama is always about conflict of some sort (which may be below the surface). Identify the conflicts in the play and you will be close to identifying the large ideas or themes which bind all the parts together.

- Make careful notes on themes, character, plot and any sub-plots of the play.

- Why do you like or dislike the characters in the play? How do your feelings towards them develop and change?

- Playwrights find non-realistic ways of allowing an audience to see into the minds and motives of their characters, for example soliloquy, aside or music. Consider how such dramatic devices are used in the play you are studying.

- Think of the playwright writing the play. Why were these particular arrangements of events, characters and speeches chosen?

- Cite exact sources for all quotations, whether from the text itself or from critical commentaries. Wherever possible find your own examples from the play to back up your opinions.

- Always express your ideas in your own words.

This York Note offers an introduction to *The Merchant of Venice* and cannot substitute for close reading of the text and the study of secondary sources.

A text of this play was first put on sale in 1600. It has always been a popular stage play, and is said to have been performed more often than any of Shakespeare's plays except *Hamlet*. It has romance and comedy; tragedy is narrowly averted; and it offers two strong character-roles in Portia and Shylock. In the trial scene at the climax, Act IV Scene 1, the wit and skill of the heroine Portia (disguised as a lawyer) save Antonio, the Merchant of Venice, from death at the hands of Shylock the Jew. Shylock is a character who has come to dominate the theatrical history of the play.

Antonio had lent his young friend Bassanio 3,000 ducats so that Bassanio could pay court to Portia, a beautiful heiress. Antonio's ships are at sea and, though a rich merchant, he had had to borrow this sum from Shylock for a term of three months. Their 'merry bond' gave Shylock the right to cut a pound from Antonio's flesh if the bond were not kept. All Antonio's ships fail to come to port, and his bond is forfeit. When Shylock's revenge is foiled by Portia, he is mercifully treated, but has to become a Christian.

Shakespeare weaves the story of the flesh-bond with another story from folklore or fairytale: the beautiful heiress who by her father's will must marry the man who chooses correctly between three caskets, of gold, silver and lead. Portia, Lady of Belmont, is the heroine of both stories. The casket scenes offer pageantry and drama, especially when Bassanio chooses the right casket.

A second romantic element is that Shylock's daughter Jessica elopes with Lorenzo, and becomes a Christian. A love scene between them introduces a last Act of moonlight and music, in which romantic confusions are magically sorted out.

But all is not sweetness and light, rescues and weddings. There are dark sides to the play, not only the threat to the life of the generous and selfless Antonio, but also in the character and situation of Shylock. He is a strongly marked, proud, powerful character, whose emotive speeches arouse audience sympathy despite his merciless conduct.

So strong is the sympathy which performance can generate for Shylock that a theatrical tradition developed in the eighteenth century in which the rescue of Antonio and the love of Portia and Bassanio were replaced as the chief focus by the figure of Shylock. Shylock's least attractive lines were cut out, and sometimes Act V was cut entirely. This rewriting of the play has sometimes led to the mistaken supposition that the

Merchant of the title must be Shylock, a more memorable figure than the quiet Antonio.

Good plays dramatise several viewpoints, and it is unwise to be positive about 'what Shakespeare meant' since his plays can be read in several ways. *The Merchant of Venice* reads well and makes a compelling stage play. The history of its interpretation is also interesting in itself. It reveals centuries of changing attitudes: to Christianity, Judaism and religion; to ideals of marriage and of noble friendship; to money, merchants and usury; and to Jews. Between 1700 and 1945, audiences in England became less prejudiced against Jews, previously regarded with suspicion as strange unbelievers or grasping moneylenders. The Nazi policy of exterminating Jews, brought to the attention even of those with no interest in public affairs, shocked non-Jews in English-speaking countries into re-appraisal: what could have led a civilised country like Germany to such a policy? Western audiences have since 1945 seen many representations, on stage and screen, in newspapers and books, of Jews as victims. This was not how Jews were seen by Shakespeare's Christian audience, taught that if Jews refused to accept Christ they could not be saved. This teaching was supplemented by legend, hearsay and prejudice, and also by a theatrical tradition in which Jews were cruel and unreal – rather like the Germans caricatured in post-war British films. In the medieval Mystery plays, Judas wore a red wig and a large nose; he was a comic villain, an object of ridicule. A ballad published in 1664 by Thomas Jordan, an old actor, suggests that Shakespeare's Shylock continued that tradition.

It is now four centuries since this play first took the stage. But at that time it had been three centuries since Londoners had seen Jews, except on the stage. For Jews had been expelled from England by King Edward I in 1290. *The Merchant of Venice* is a rich and successful play, full of character and incident, comedy and poetry, building up to an intensely dramatic trial and a brilliantly contrived happy ending. But the play is also a cultural document and a theatrical phenomenon whose subsequent life reveals profound changes in Western cultural attitudes between 1600 and 2000.

# PART TWO

# SUMMARIES

Shakespeare's play was first performed in 1596–8, probably in 1597. A text of *The Merchant of Venice* was printed in 1600 in quarto format, with a title page reading:

> The most excellent History [i.e., story] of the *Merchant of Venice*. With the extreame crueltie of *Shylocke* the Iewe towards the sayd Merchant, in cutting a iust pound of his fleshe: and the obtayning of *Portia* by the choyse of three chests. *As it hath beene divers times acted by the Lord Chamberlaine his servants.*
>
> Written by William Shakespeare.

The first performances by Shakespeare's company would have been at The Theatre. The Globe did not open until 1599.

A second quarto appeared in 1619; a third text appeared in the 1623 collection of thirty-six of Shakespeare's plays in the large folio format. The 1623 volume is known as the First Folio; three further folio editions appeared in the seventeenth century. (Quarto is a small format, like a modern paperback text of a single play; folio, a massive volume.) The three early texts of the play are substantially the same, fortunately, and modern texts have very few differences; one is over the character Salarino (see below). Modern editions number the lines differently, however, especially the lines of prose, for the number of words in a line depends on print size and page width. It is thought that the quarto was printed from a fair copy of Shakespeare's manuscript, and that the folio was based on the quarto, though it adds stage directions, probably from a prompt book. Act divisions were added to the plays in the folio edition; numbered scenes were added by Rowe, who edited the plays in 1714.

Most of the many trivial differences in modern texts arise from the different ways in which editors modernise Elizabethan spelling and punctuation. Some editors add further stage directions. They also standardise the names of characters prefixed to each speech. Thus Shylock is usually 'Iew(e)' [Jew] in quarto and folio, but modern editors regularise this to 'Shylock'.

Both quarto and folio editions have three characters, Salarino, Salerio and Solanio, but most modern editors think that Salarino disappeared into the character of Salerio in a revision of the play. Salarino is therefore found only in Mahood's edition and in that of Halio.

The text used for this edition is M.M. Mahood, New Cambridge Shakespeare, Cambridge University Press, 1987, although it is not assumed that the reader has any particular edition.

For comments on other editions of *The Merchant of Venice*, see Further Reading.

## SYNOPSIS

The play combines two stories, the flesh-bond tale and the love-caskets tale. Bassanio wishes to offer marriage to Portia, the heiress of Belmont, but cannot compete with her other suitors. She is the heiress of a great fortune, but her father's will provides that she can marry only the man who chooses the casket (there are three, of gold, silver and lead) which contains her portrait.

Bassanio uses the credit of his good friend Antonio (the Merchant of Venice) to borrow 3,000 ducats from the Jewish moneylender Shylock, who hates Antonio. Antonio promises to pay the money back in three months or to allow Shylock to cut a pound of flesh from near his heart; the bond is sealed.

In Belmont, after the princes of Morocco and Arragon have chosen the wrong caskets of gold and of silver, Bassanio chooses rightly, and Portia gives him a ring which makes him her lord, and he engages never to part with it. Her gentlewoman Nerissa likewise becomes engaged to Gratiano, who wears her ring on the same terms.

All Antonio's ships are lost and his bond is forfeit. At the trial, Bassanio (who now has Portia's money) offers to repay it several times over, but Shylock wants his pound of flesh according to the bond. He sharpens his knife. The Duke hands the trial over to a young judge, Balthazar (Portia in disguise). After Shylock refuses mercy, she awards the case to him; but stipulates that no drop of blood be spilt, since that is not mentioned in the bond. Shylock asks for the money instead, but has been awarded his pound of flesh and nothing else. If he takes more or less than a pound he must die.

He withdraws, but Balthazar-Portia invokes the law of Venice that no alien shall plot against the life of a citizen. The penalty is death, with confiscation of goods, half to the intended victim, half to the State.

The Duke spares Shylock's life, and will accept a fine rather than half of Shylock's goods. Antonio asks the Duke to let Shylock off all the state's half, and takes his half in trust for Shylock's daughter Jessica (who has eloped with a Christian, Lorenzo). There are two conditions: that Shylock becomes a Christian and leaves all his goods to his son-in-law and daughter. Shylock accepts.

Bassanio offers Balthazar-Portia payment, which she declines, asking instead for the ring. Bassanio refuses, but at Antonio's suggestion sends the ring after Balthazar-Portia. Nerissa plays the same trick on Gratiano. The ladies get back to Belmont first, and ask the men for the rings which they had given them. They berate them, then explain the joke and forgive them. Antonio's wealth is restored, and the play ends with Portia and Bassanio, Nerissa and Gratiano, and Lorenzo and Jessica about to begin their marriages.

## ACT I

### SCENE 1 Venice: Bassanio asks Antonio, the Merchant of Venice, for a loan so that he can court Portia. Antonio offers Bassanio his credit to borrow the money

Antonio denies the suggestion of his younger friends that he is sad because he is worried about his ships. Alone with his 'noble kinsman' Bassanio, Antonio asks about Bassanio's secret pilgrimage. Bassanio says he has wasted the money that Antonio had advanced him; Antonio offers to help again. Embarrassed, Bassanio explains that he needs money in order to compete as a suitor with the grandees who seek the hand of Portia of Belmont, a blonde heiress of fabulous beauty and fortune. As Antonio's money is invested in ventures at sea, he offers Bassanio the use of his, Antonio's, name as credit for a loan in Venice.

> The high courtesy of Venetian society derives from the wealth carried in private ships; images of great merchant ships decorate the conversation.

Antonio is quiet, in contrast with his talkative young followers. His friend Bassanio speaks with painful elaboration until he finds that his prodigal waste of money has not affected Antonio's love.

Fortune is established as a theme: with Antonio's help, Bassanio's suit to Portia will be 'fortunate'; as Antonio's 'fortunes are at sea', his credit will unfortunately have to do.

**want-wit** fool

**argosies** private cargo-vessels (from Ragusa, now Dubrovnik)

**signors** noble rulers of Venice

**Piring** looking closely

**Andrew** ship as rich as the San Andrès, captured in Cadiz in 1596 and renamed the *Andrew*

**Vailing** bowing

**bottom** hull, cargo ship

**Janus** Roman god of doorways, two-faced

**peep through their eyes** because half-closed with laughter

**bagpiper** maker of sad music

**Nestor** the wisest and oldest of the Greeks

**respect upon** regard for

**alabaster** fine stone used for figures on tombs

**cream and mantle** become opaque

**standing** stagnant

**gudgeon** a fish easily caught

**gear** matter, occasion

**neat's tongue dried** ox-tongue cured for eating

**vendible** saleable, i.e. marriageable

**swelling port** proud deportment

**abridged** reduced

**rate** lifestyle

**or ... Or** either ... or

**Brutus' Portia** a noble Roman woman

**golden fleece** fleece of a golden sheep, the legendary prize sought by Jason and his Argonauts on the shores (**strand**) of Colchis in the Black Sea

**of my trust** on my credit

SCENE 2    **Belmont: Portia's situation. Portia and Nerissa discuss Portia's father's will, by which she will marry. Portia reviews her suitors and favours Bassanio**

Portia is wealthy but weary: she cannot choose her husband but is to be 'chosen' by the suitor who chooses correctly between three caskets. Her gentlewoman says that the test Portia's father has devised will find a man wise enough to be worthy of her love. The six suitors who have withdrawn are caricatures of national types; Bassanio is an ideal Renaissance man; the new suitors include the dark Prince of Morocco.

Portia's weariness echoes Antonio's sadness: does wealth or love bring happiness?

Prose sense about love at Belmont contrasts with high-sounding poetry about money in Venice.

Some of this early scene is **exposition** (the giving of information needful to the story): we learn of the will by which Portia's father has determined her marriage.

Though accepting her father's will, Portia is hard to please – until Bassanio is mentioned.

**sentences**  maxims
**divine**  theologian
**hot temper**  ardent temperament
**who chooses his meaning**  who chooses Portia's father's meaning
**level**  take aim
**Neapolitan**  Southern Italians were famous horsemen
**played false**  deceived (her husband)
**County Palatine**  Count of one of the Palatine regions of Europe (Palatine: belonging to the palace)
**And you will not have me**  if you will not have me
**Falconbridge**  a character from Shakespeare's own *King John*, a typical Englishman abroad, who speaks only his own language yet dresses in everyone else's styles
**come into the court**  bear witness
**round hose**  padded breeches
**borrowed**  received

**sealed under for another**  agreed to stand as security for another blow
**Rhenish**  from the Rhineland
**Sibylla**  a Sybil was an ageless prophetess
**Diana**  goddess of chastity
**shrive**  absolve in confession. Whatever his character, Portia does not want him for a husband
**wooer**  rhymes with **door**

SCENE 3    **Venice: Shylock agrees to lend Bassanio 3,000 ducats, which Antonio binds himself to repay in three months, or forfeit a pound of his flesh**

Shylock hears Bassanio's request, considers whether Antonio's ships will come home; asks to speak to Antonio, but declines to eat with Christians. Shylock hates Antonio because he is a Christian, and also because he lends money gratis. He makes Antonio repeat the terms. Shylock defends usury by Jacob's example; Antonio does not accept the analogy.

Trickery is established as a theme. Shylock asks why he should lend money to one who has spat upon him. Antonio is prepared to pay a penalty. Shylock, instead of interest, proposes the bond of a pound of flesh. Antonio agrees to be bound.

> Character-identification: Shylock's 'ducats' immediately identify him as a moneylender (cf. openings of previous scenes). He is also distinguished by his speech: repetition ('monies' in lines 100–21), and alien idioms. How will the director make him look, dress, behave?

> Shylock's 'Antonio is a *good* man' assesses him as a credit risk; Bassanio takes 'good' to be an opinion on Antonio's character. Such *misunderstandings* show different assumptions and values. Shylock is first a loan-shark; then (line 26) a Jew. His religious hatred (lines 34–48) is conveyed in **asides** (a theatre convention: words spoken to the audience, inaudible to those on the stage, as in lines 33 and 48) to show his secretiveness. He then displays his feelings, provoking Antonio; shows him 'kindness', revealing only later the 'merry bond' which gives him his chance of revenge.

**ducats**  gold coins (of the Duke or Doge)
**For the which ... bound**  committed in writing

**stead** help

**pleasure** oblige

**sufficient** financially acceptable as security

**in supposition** presumed

**Tripolis** Lebanese port

**the Indies** India

**Rialto** the business centre of Venice (*not* the Rialto Bridge)

**assured ... assured** reassured ... financially secured

**the Nazarite** Jesus of Nazareth, who expelled the demons possessing two men; the demons rushed into a herd of pigs (Matthew 8:28). Jews are forbidden by religious law to eat pork; and regard Jesus as no more than a prophet

**fawning publican** in the Gospels, publicans are Jewish tax-collectors for the Romans and therefore traitors. Jesus included publicans among his friends. Antonio is 'fawning' because he comes to beg of Shylock. But Christ tells a parable favourably contrasting the humility before God of a publican with the arrogance of a Pharisee (Luke 18:9–14). The phrase has different implications for Jews and for Christians

**usance** euphemism for usury (cf. lines 42–3)

**upon the hip** (wrestling term) at a disadvantage

**thrift** (euphemism for interest) thriving

**my tribe** the Jewish people (not one of the twelve tribes of Israel)

**store** wealth

**gross** full sum

**But soft** wait!

**in our mouths** we were speaking of

**Upon advantage** to your own profit

**use** practise (with perhaps a dig at 'usance' (line 37 above))

**Jacob** Jacob *alias* Israel had twelve sons, ancestors of the twelve tribes of Israel (see Historical Background). As son of Isaac and grandson of **Abra(ha)m**, Jacob was the **third possessor** of the birthright of Abraham, but only through the work of **his wise mother**, Rebecca, who helped him trick the blind old Isaac into granting it to Jacob rather than to his elder (twin) brother Esau. To flee Esau's rage Jacob served his uncle **Laban** for seven years in order to win his daughter Rachel; but Laban tricked him into marrying his eldest daughter Leah. Jacob paid Laban back by getting him to agree that he could keep any sheep and goats born spotted; Jacob then increased their number by a trick of his own

**compromised** agreed

**eanlings** new-born lambs

**hire** payment

**rank** in heat, ready for sexual intercourse

**work of generation** breeding

**pilled me** peeled; **me** a colloquial 'ethical dative' adding nothing to the sense

**wands** sticks

**deed of kind** mating

**fulsome** pregnant (it was believed that offspring resembled what the mother was looking at when she conceived)

**eaning** bearing

**Fall** produce

**venture** risk (Antonio distinguishes between his venture capitalism involving effort, risk and providence, and Shylock's usury – see Historical Background, on Usury)

**inserted** brought in (by Shylock)

**Or is your gold ... rams?** a rhetorical question expecting the answer no, for money does not multiply by nature

**note me** listen (Antonio has turned aside)

**rated** berated

**Still have I** I have always

**gaberdine** loose cloak

**void your rheum** spit

**A breed ... metal** a profit from increase of metal, which does not reproduce in the way of living creatures

**break** become bankrupt

**doit** a small Dutch coin of little value

**kind** natural kindness

**This were kindness** This would indeed be kindness

**single** simple, unconditional

**merry sport** joke

**nominated** named

**equal** exact

**seal** give my seal (impress it in wax)

**fearful** untrustworthy

**gentle** (pun) kind / Gentile, repeated throughout the play

**Belmont: Morocco learns the terms**

Portia says she is not put off by Morocco's dark skin. The proud Prince agrees never to marry if he should choose the wrong casket.

> *Exoticism* is a theme of the play. Venice (see Historical Background) is exotic and Belmont is more so. The Prince's words emphasise his darkness, prowess and pride. Dress would show Morocco as the most exotic of the suitors. (Venice employed Moors as soldiers to defend her Mediterranean empire; Shakespeare's *Othello* is subtitled *The Moor of Venice*. Moors had the glamour of an enemy who is no longer dangerous, unlike the Turks.)

**flourish** short call

**cornets** woodwind horns

**tawny** light-skinned (unlike a 'blackamoor')

**livery** distinctive clothing

**near bred** brought up

**Phoebus' fire** heat of the (god of the) sun

**incision** cut

**feared** frightened

**nice** fastidious

**scanted** restricted

**Sophy** the Shah of Persia

**Solyman** Suleiman the Magnificent, Sultan of Turkey

**a roars** he roars

**Lichas** servant who brought Hercules a poisoned shirt, and was thrown into the sea in his **rage**

**Alcides** the Greek name of Hercules

**be advised** think it over

SCENE 2 **Venice: Lancelot Gobbo and his father**

The clown Lancelot Gobbo resolves to leave Shylock's service. He fools about with his blind old father. Bassanio agrees to take on Lancelot as a servant. He orders a feast for the evening. Graziano promises to be quiet if he is allowed to accompany Bassanio to Belmont.

> Lancelot, the Clown or professional comedian, makes out that he is torn between 'conscience' and 'the fiend' (Devil), like a character in an

old Morality Play. He is modelled on the Vice, a comic attendant on the Devil in those plays. His comic patter is full of meaningless phrases, repetition, confusion and **malapropism** (using the wrong word). His role is to make the audience laugh, although not everything in his patter is nonsense. In Italian *gobbo* means 'hunchback', a figure of Venetian folklore.

**pack** go
**Fia!** away! (Italian *via*)
**neck of my heart** anatomically absurd phrase
**smack ... taste** sexually suggestive words
**God ... mark!** routine apology before something indelicate (cf. modern 'Pardon my French'), like **saving your reverence** (lines 19–20)
**incarnation** (malapropism) incarnate
**true-begotten** (malapropism) true-begetter
**sand-blind** nearly blind
**high gravel-blind** more nearly blind (a Gobbo-ism)
**confusions** (malapropism) conclusions; to 'try conclusions' was to try or prove an experiment or to propose riddles
**Be God's sonties** by God's saints
**the waters** a storm (of tears)
**'master'** the title of one who has (rather than is) a servant
**well to live** in good health
***ergo*** therefore (Latin, used by the learned)
**sisters three** the classical Fates
**staff of my age** biblical phrase
**hovel-post** prop for a shelter
**father** old man
**a wise father** Gobbo reverses the old proverb
**[*Kneels*]** traditional **stage business** (physical actions accompanying the words) is for the son to kneel facing the wrong way so that at line 77 old Gobbo feels his son's hair instead of his chin
**Give me your blessing** Jacob's request to Isaac, prompted by his 'wise mother' (I.3.65)
**thou** a change from the respectful 'you'
**fill-horse** draught-horse
**set up my rest** bet my bottom dollar

**very Jew** a real miser
**halter** hangman's noose
**tell every ... ribs** reversing the usual saying
**a Jew** which I am not (cf. 'I'm a Dutchman')
**Gramercy** from French '(May God) grant (you) mercy'
**infection** (malapropism) affection, desire
**cater-cousins** cousins who entertain each other
**frutify** (malapropism?) notify
**dish of doves** a humble countryman's present
**impertinent** (malapropism) pertinent
**defect** (malapropism) effect, upshot
**preferred** recommended
**old proverb** 'The grace of God is enough'
**parted** divided
**guarded** ornamented (perhaps as a Fool)
**I cannot get** Lancelot is boasting that he *can*
**table** palm (placed on a Bible)
**small trifle** (irony) fortune-telling by palm-reading indicates Lancelot's prodigious luck in marriage (cf. that of his new master)
**coming-in** only a beginning
**featherbed** i.e., marriage is more dangerous than a voyage at sea
**scapes** adventures
**gear** occasion
**twinkling** of an eye: a moment
**rude** outspoken
**liberal** easy-going
**misconstered** misconstrued
**sad ostent** grave outward show

## SCENE 3    Venice: Jessica's letter to Lorenzo

Jessica gives Lancelot a letter for Lorenzo, with whom she will elope and become a Christian.

The last piece setting up the plot is introduced rapidly and simply, though attention is drawn to Jessica's lack of filial feeling. The final couplet (pair of rhyming lines) gives a clear signal to the future.

**exhibit** (pair of malapropism) inhibit

## SCENE 4    Venice: Lorenzo's plan of elopement

Lorenzo receives Jessica's letter and bids Lancelot tell Jessica that he will not fail her. Lorenzo tells Gratiano of the plan of elopement: Jessica will be disguised as a boy torchbearer at the supper.

This scene runs on from the last. It repeats the Christian justification for Jessica's elopement

**Disguise** for the masque at supper
**quaintly** skilfully
**break up** unseal
**the hand** the handwriting
**By your leave** excuse me
**Unless she do it** unless misfortune does it
**That she is** that Jessica is
**faithless** without Christian faith

## SCENE 5    Venice: Shylock bids Jessica lock up

As he leaves the house for supper, Shylock bids his daughter lock up while he is out, especially when he hears that there will be a masque at Bassanio's supper. Lancelot gives her Lorenzo's message.

Contrast Shylock's miserliness towards his former servant with his own willingness to grow fat at the expense of Christian wasters. Shylock is made to forget that he will not eat with Christians (I.3.30); has Shakespeare forgotten, or has Shylock changed his mind?

There is much made of the supper and the masque, but this seems to serve chiefly as a diversion of Shylock's attention. Although Shylock's attendance allows Jessica to escape, he could have been made to sleep through it. Does the elaborate locking-up serve a dramatic purpose?

**What, Jessica!** a sharp summons, repeated
**rend apparel out** rip clothing; perhaps letting it out because Lancelot was getting fat?
**could do ... bidding** (pun) would do nothing without being called / would accomplish nothing without calling (others)
**Look to** guard

**rest** (pun) peace / hoard
**dream of money bags** i.e., that he would *lose* money, since dreams were
supposed to go by opposites
**tonight** last night
**reproach** for 'approach'? ('reproach' also fits)
**conspired** Lancelot is indiscreet
**Black Monday** Easter Monday. Nose-bleeds were bad luck; a rigmarole
mocking Shylock's dream-lore
**varnished** (pun) masked / drunken
**Jacob's staff** Jacob left for Laban's with only a staff and returned a rich man;
an example of 'thrift'
**worth a Jewès eye** worth a Jew's inspection, hence a rich gem
**that ... Hagar's offspring** a line full of tribal resentment. To Shylock, Christians
are outcasts, having left the house of Israel; and thus are sons of Hagar.
Hagar, Abraham's concubine, fled his house complaining of harsh treatment
(cf. Lancelot and Jessica). Hagar's son was Ishmael, a mocker, like Lancelot
**patch** fool

### SCENE 6   Venice: Jessica elopes with Lorenzo

Lorenzo joins his masked friends by Shylock's house; Jessica throws him a
casket and joins him, dressed as a boy. Antonio says Bassanio's ship is ready
to depart.

Gratiano's memorable comment on young love is given prominence
just before we see the elopement. Why?

Why does Shakespeare have Jessica throw Lorenzo a casket, and why
does she further 'gild' herself?

**penthouse** shelter with sloping roof
**the clock** the time of their meeting
**pigeons** doves drawing the chariot of Venus
**unforfeited** unbroken (newly betrothed lovers are keener than faithful spouses
to keep their word)
**younger** the Prodigal was a younger son (Luke 15:11–32). Some editors
prefer the spelling **younker**, a young nobleman
**scarfèd bark** beflagged ship (of love)
**strumpet** prostitute (cf. the harlots with whom the Prodigal wastes his
substance, inviting but false)

**overweathered ribs**  worn timbers
**abode**  stay
**my father Jew**  my Jewish father-in-law
**catch this casket**  (cf. the catching of Portia via a casket)
**exchange**  change of role: girl-boy/daughter-wife
**office of discovery**  job which is to uncover
**lovely garnish**  lovely outward trappings
**gild**  cover thinly with gold
**moe**  a greater number of
**gentle**  (pun) generous / gentile
**gentleman**  i.e., Jessica
**No masque ... come about**  a switch of plan

scene **7**    **Belmont: Morocco fails**

Morocco chooses the golden casket, proud to gain 'that which many men desire'. Inside is a skull.

The scene begins and opens with stage directions, from Portia: 'draw aside the curtains' – the curtains hide the caskets, which in turn hide the fate of her suitors.

Proud Morocco goes for gold and finds death. Does this bear on the play's themes?

**discover**  uncover
**several**  different
**all as blunt**  quite as unappealing (as lead)
**hazard**  venture
**withal**  too
**virgin hue**  colour of the moon/Diana/chastity
**an even hand**  impartially
**estimation**  repute
**mortal breathing**  living (unlike the saint in a shrine)
**Hyrcanian**  south of the Caspian sea
**To rib ... cerecloth**  enclose (in lead) her waxed shroud
**tried**  assayed, purified
**angel**  the archangel St Michael
**insculped upon**  engraved on top of

**A carrion death**  dead figure of Death: skull
**inscrolled**  written on this scroll
**suit is cold**  proverb announcing failure
**welcome frost**  hello to single life
**A gentle riddance!**  a pleasing departure

SCENE 8   Venice: Bassanio has sailed

Shylock raises the alarm: daughter and ducats are gone, he suspects with Bassanio. We hear that one of Antonio's ships is lost, and of his grief at parting with Bassanio.

A scene of **exposition** reported in conversation.

It is made clear Jessica was not in Bassanio's ship; Antonio and Bassanio play no part in her abduction.

Antonio's feelings at losing first a ship and then Bassanio are to be compared with Shylock's reaction to the loss of his ducats and his daughter.

What conclusions should we draw?

It is now clear that Antonio loves Bassanio.

**given to understand**  led to believe
**daughter**  the 'ght' may have been pronounced
**Christian ducats**  won from Christians and now lost to them
**double ducats**  two-ducat coins
**his stones**  (pun) jewels / testicles
**keep his day**  pay up on the appointed day
**reasoned**  talked
**Slubber**  perform in a slovenly way
**stay ... riping**  wait for the ripest moment
**mind of love**  thoughts when contemplating love
**ostents**  demonstrations
**conveniently**  appropriately
**affection ... sensible**  emotion strangely evident
**he only loves ... him**  i.e., Bassanio is all he lives for
**quicken ... heaviness**  lighten the grief he hugs to him

SCENE 9    Belmont: Arragon fails

Arragon chooses the silver casket to 'get as much as he deserves'. Inside is a fool's head. News of the arrival of Bassanio excites Portia.

Arragon has the arrogance suggested by his name. He is Prince of Aragon, part of Spain, which was the great power of Europe, ruler of southern Italy and enemy to England.

He chooses not what many men desire but what he believes he deserves: 'I will assume desert.' He scorns the fool multitude and gets a fool's head.

Portia's readiness to love Bassanio is again made very clear.

**Servitor** servant
**straight** immediately
**election** choice
**addressed me** prepared myself
**be meant By** refer to
**fond** foolish
**martlet** house-martin
**force ... casualty** power and path of accident
**jump with** join
**cozen** deceive
**derived** obtained
**clear honour** noble honour
**cover** keep their hats on
**gleaned** discarded (from harvested corn)
**new varnished** dusted and made bright again
**schedule** scroll
**judge** to judge
**offices** roles
**shadows** phantoms, likenesses
**iwis** for sure
**Silvered o'er** covered in silver (decorations worn by court officials)
**Take what wife** 'Perhaps the poet had forgotten that he who missed Portia was never to marry any woman' (Dr Johnson)
**head** you will always be like me (a fool)

**sped**  dealt with
**wroth**  wrath, anger
**deliberate**  deliberating
**They have ... to lose**  they have enough intelligence to choose wrongly
**my lord**  you, sir (a little joke)
**Venetian**  i.e., Gratiano
**sensible regreets**  tangible greetings (see line 90)
**costly**  gorgeous
**forespurrer**  one who rides before
**highday**  feast day, celebratory
**post**  messenger
**Bassanio ... will it be!**  O Cupid, let it be Bassanio!

# ACT III

## SCENE 1  Venice: Shylock resolves to have revenge

Antonio's friends lament the loss of his ship, laugh at Shylock's loss of his daughter. Tubal reports that Jessica is squandering Shylock's money; and that another of Antonio's ships is lost. Shylock resolves to 'have the heart' of Antonio.

More **exposition** by Antonio's talkative friends.

Losses are balanced: Shylock's daughter, Antonio's ship.

Shylock's 'Let him look to his bond', thrice repeated, warns that his motive (despite his speech on the common humanity of Jew and Christian) is revenge.

The cruelty of Gentile mockery should not conceal the fact that the father does indeed seem to miss ducats more than daughter.

The effect of Tubal's alternation of bad and good news is to torture Shylock. Tubal's news confirms Shylock's desire to torture Antonio.

Is Tubal unmotivated, comic?

**unchecked**  uncontradicted
**Goodwins**  the Goodwin Sands at the mouth of the Thames
**knapped**  munched

**slips**  counterfeits

**crossing**  deviating from

**full stop**  conclusion

**betimes**  quickly

**cross**  spoil

**wings**  i.e., the clothes of a page

**fledged**  fit to fly

**complexion**  disposition

**old carrion**  you old corpse

**Rebels it**  does it rebel (in having a 'disobedient' erection)? (Solanio pretends to misunderstand)

**Rhenish**  a fine (white) wine from the Rhine

**match**  bargain, deal

**look to**  keep

**forfeit**  fail, incur the penalty

**bait**  use as bait for

**dimensions**  parts

**affections**  reactions

**what is his humility?**  what form does his humility take?

**what … sufferance**  what form should his forbearance take

**it shall go hard but**  assuredly

**matched**  found equal

**curse**  Christ's prophecy of the destruction of Jerusalem

**hearsed**  laid out

**No news of them**  i.e., of the jewels

**for a monkey**  to buy a monkey

**of Leah**  from Leah (his wife)

**fee me**  hire for me

**synagogue**  perhaps to swear the oath of IV.1.225

SCENE 2   **Belmont: Bassanio's joy and grief**

Portia is anxious, but Bassanio chooses the lead casket containing Portia's portrait. They rejoice; she gives him a ring which he must keep. Gratiano and Nerissa also become engaged. Lorenzo brings a letter from Antonio: his ships are lost, his bond is forfeit. Bassanio goes to him.

Portia is seriously in love, yet her second speech (lines 40–62) is fanciful and **mock-heroic** (using heroic comparisons, e.g., 'Go, Hercules', for playful purposes).

Apart from initial *flourishes* on the cornets, the song 'Tell me where is fancy bred' is the first music in the play. Its connection of music with love is developed in Act V.

The engagement of Portia and Bassanio is golden; Gratiano's engagement repeats the tune in a lower, brassier key.

The bad news changes the notes to tragic, but Bassanio still speaks of engagements (lines 260–1).

**quality**  manner
**Beshrew**  a mild curse
**if mine then yours**  because husband and wife are one flesh
**these naughty times**  this worthless age
**peize**  weigh down, slow down
**eche**  eke out
**election**  choosing
**rack**  i.e., of time. Instrument of torture on which traitors were stretched to make them confess
**fear**  fear for
**enforcèd**  under torture
**aloof**  apart
**swan-like**  it was believed that the mute swan sang before dying
**flourish**  fanfare
**presence**  dignity
**Alcides**  Hercules, who rescued a beautiful virgin from the sea-monster. As reward, he asked for Laomedon's famous horses rather than the girl (hence 'with much more love'). A tale from Ovid's *Metamorphoses*
**howling**  weeping
**stand for sacrifice**  am ready to die
**Dardanian wives**  Trojan women
**blearèd**  tear-stained
**Live thou**  should you live
**fancy**  fantasy, sexual attraction
**cradle**  in its infancy in the eye
**So may ... themselves**  may outward appearances fade away (Bassanio's

thoughts as he looks at the caskets echo those of the song)
**still** ever
**stayers** ropes
**livers white as milk** a bloodless liver was a sign of cowardice
**excrement** growth, i.e., a beard
**redoubted** feared
**purchased ... weight** (cosmetics) bought by the ounce
**lightest** most fickle and faithless
**supposèd** what is thought
**dowry ... head** legacy of another's head
**guilèd** treacherous
**Indian** dusky (not fair, not beautiful)
**Hard ... Midas** everything Midas touched turned to gold, including his food. From the *Metamorphoses*
**drudge** slave (silver; common coinage)
**meagre** poor
**paleness** lack of colour
**As** such as
**scant** ration
**counterfeit** picture
**golden mesh** a hair-net of gold wire
**How could he see** (when blinded by her eyes)
**continent** that which contains
**Chance as fair** hazard as fortunately
**by note** as instructed
**Exceed account** love's blessings are uncountable
**vantage to exclaim on** opportunity to accuse
**none from me** none to be unavailable to me (i.e., for there is plenty of joy to go round)
**so thou canst get** as long as you can get
**intermission** idle time
**sweat** sweated
**roof** i.e., of the mouth
**play** wager
**stake down ... stake down** put down the money now ... with a limp penis
**youth** recentness
**interest** influence

SCENE 2 continued

**very friends** true friends
**My purpose ... here** it was not my purpose to have seen you here
**Commends ... you** sends you his greetings
**estate** state, condition
**stranger** newcomer, i.e., Jessica
**royal** superlative
**Jasons** see Act I.1.169
**fleece** (pun) fleets
**shrewd** painful
**Ran in my veins** was my (gentle) blood
**engaged** pledged
**mere** absolute
**hit** succeeded
**Barbary** North Africa (land of the Berbers)
**should appear** seems
**confound** destroy
**impeach** discredit
**freedom** legal protection
**envious** malicious
**deface** cancel
**use your pleasure** follow your inclination

## SCENE 3   Venice: Antonio expects death

Shylock refuses to listen to Antonio: he is determined to have his bond, relying on the strict law of Venice. Antonio hopes Bassanio will come before he dies.

The scene makes evident the intensity of Shylock's vengefulness and establishes Antonio's patient resignation.

**naughty** worthless
**kept** dwelt
**bootless** unprofitable
**forfeitures** penalties for breach of contract
**Therefore** that is why
**commodity** access to our privileges
**Consisteth of** relies upon the equal standing of
**so bated me** made me so thin

SCENE 4    **Belmont: Portia follows Bassanio**

Portia leaves her estate in the hands of Lorenzo and Jessica, while she withdraws to a convent. She sends a messenger to her cousin Dr Bellario in Padua, and tells Nerissa that they are to adopt male disguise.

Lorenzo establishes the Renaissance idea of noble male friendship as 'god-like'. Portia's acceptance of this prompts her generosity throughout the play.

The women's disguise as men, and the fiction of the convent, are conventions of romantic comedy.

**conceit** conception
**amity** (Platonic) friendship (see Themes, on Love, Marriage and Friendship)
**Than customary ... you** than your usual generosity can make you
**waste** spend
**lineaments** characteristics
**bosom lover** intimate friend and confidant
**In purchasing ... soul** in redeeming my soul's image, i.e., Bassanio's friend
**state of hellish cruelty** hell of victimhood
**husbandry and manage** care and management
**imposition** charge
**imagined speed** the speed of imagination
**traject** ferry (Italian *traghetto)*
**that we lack** i.e., masculine characteristics
**'frays** affrays, fights
**quaint** elaborate
**do withal** help it
**raw** immature
**jacks** knaves
**turn to** turn into (not, as Portia pretends, 'turn towards', though this must be in the minds of newly weds whose wedding night has been postponed)
**If thou ... interpreter** if overheard by someone who thought it indecent
**device** plan

SCENE 5    Belmont: Lancelot, Jessica and Lorenzo

Jessica is now a Christian; she and her husband praise Portia and Lord Bassanio.

Lancelot's fooling should not conceal the serious contention that stealing her away is justified by the salvation of her soul.

Lorenzo again extols Portia's nobility, and although he and Jessica end jokingly, many a true word is spoken in jest in this play.

**the sins of the father** quoted from the second of the Ten Commandments given to Moses; referring to Shylock
**fear you** fear for you
**agitation** for 'cogitation'?
**bastard** ill-founded
**neither** anyway
**got** begot
**sins of my mother** i.e., of adultery, in conceiving Jessica outside wedlock
**Scylla ... Charybdis** In Homer's *Odyssey*, Ulysses had to steer between the monster Scylla and the whirlpool of Charybdis in the straits between Italy and Sicily. This old proverb is turned by Lancelot into a joke against Shylock/Scylla (similar in sound) and Jessica's mother, whom he could 'fall into'
**I shall be saved by my husband** 'The unbelieving wife is sanctified by the husband' (I Cor. 7:14)
**enow** enough (an economic joke: if pork-eaters outnumber pigs, bacon prices will rise)
**a rasher** bacon
**are out** i.e., of corners and of sympathy
**commonwealth** society
**Moor** a black attendant on Morocco?
**more than reason** bigger than reasonable
**less than ... honest** unchaste
**more** (pun) better
**sirrah** sir (used in rebuke to a servant)
**stomachs** appetites
**'cover'** lay the table
**duty** i.e., not to cover (my head with a hat)

**occasion** opportunity to make a pun
**humours and conceits** inclinations and fancies
**O dear discretion** what fine discrimination!
**Garnished** equipped
**Defy the matter** avoid the point
**lay** bet
**Pawned** added as a stake
**set you forth** praise you

# ACT IV

SCENE 1   Venice: the trial scene. Shylock insists on his bond. Portia
(disguised as an advocate) is made judge in the case. Shylock
refuses mercy and insists on justice according to his bond.
She awards him the penalty – but he must not take a drop of
blood, or more or less than a pound of flesh, on penalty of
death. Shylock is foiled. Portia invokes another law by
which an alien who has tried to kill a Venetian must lose his
life and his property. Shylock is let off both penalties, on
conditions: that he become a Christian; and leave his money
to Lorenzo and Jessica. The only payment Portia will accept
from Bassanio is his ring

Antonio patiently awaits his fate. Shylock refuses the Duke's plea for
clemency and Bassanio's offer of twice the money, and whets his knife.
Nerissa, dressed as a lawyer's clerk, brings a letter from the lawyer Bellario
to the Duke, commending a young doctor Balthasar (Portia in disguise) to
try the case.

Portia commends mercy to Shylock, who demands justice. She gives
judgment in his favour, according to the bond, and Antonio bids farewell
to Bassanio. Portia warns Shylock not to take a drop of blood, which is not
in the bond. He now tries to take Bassanio's earlier offer but this is
disallowed; he is due exactly one pound of flesh. He asks for the 3,000
ducats, but can have his bond only. He tries to leave, but Portia accuses him
as an alien of seeking the life of a Venetian. The penalty is to pay half his
goods to the Venetian, the other half to the State, while his life is in forfeit
to the Duke.

The Duke grants him his life and offers to mitigate the State's share. Antonio asks the Duke to waive the State's share, and says he will hold his half-share in trust for Lorenzo and Jessica, provided Shylock becomes a Christian and leaves his estate to Lorenzo and Jessica. Shylock accepts.

Balthazar-Portia has to leave urgently. She refuses Bassanio's offer of payment but asks for his ring. He refuses, but when urged by Antonio sends it after her.

The content of this scene is discussed in Textual Analysis, Text 2.

The following comments relate to its dramatic structure.

Shylock's answer to why he wants his pound of flesh (lines 35–62) is insulting; it also shows how far he is in the grip of hatred.

He stands on his rights, making an analogy with the legal rights of Christian slave-holders (lines 89–103) which exposes Christian hypocrisy.

Shylock's knife and scales add symbolic meaning as well as drama. He believes in law and sacrifice.

Portia speaks for mercy, but denies Bassanio's plea that the law be relaxed, since the letter of the law offers her her only opportunity.

The Duke and Antonio show mercy and magnanimity to a defeated foe, in contrast to Gratiano's insults.

The moral blackmail used by Portia to get her ring back succeeds because of Antonio's sense of obligation.

**Magnificoes** judges elected by the nobility
**qualify** moderate
**envy** malice
**but lead'st ... fashion** only maintain this pretence
**last hour of act** last moment before performance
**remorse more strange** more wonderful pity
**loose** surrender
**moiety** half
**Turks ... Tartars** who do not share the religious traditions which Jews have in common with Christians

**possessed** informed

**sworn** presumably in the synagogue at the end of Act III Scene 1

**charter** a mistake: Venice did not have a charter from the Crown, as an English city would

**humour** predisposition resulting from the balance of bodily fluids; cf. the loose modern use of 'allergy'

**baned** poisoned

**affection** physical reaction

**lodged** fixed

**losing** (for he would lose 3,000 ducats)

**think** remember

**main flood bate** high tide decrease

**How shalt ... mercy** cf. James 2:13 'For there shall be judgement merciless to him that showeth no mercy'

**many a purchased slave** i.e., in Venice. But Shylock has a general point: slavery was practised throughout Christian Europe including England

**I stand for judgement** cf. IV.1.142 and Portia at III.2.57 and Antonio at IV.1

**Upon** by

**determine** settle

**one drop of blood** (an unremarked prophecy)

**tainted wether** a diseased castrated ram. Abraham substituted a ram provided by God for Isaac (Genesis 22:13)

**whet** sharpen

**inexecrable** beyond cursing

**faith** Christian belief, incompatible with those of Pythagoras

**To hold opinion with** to agree

**Pythagoras** early Greek philosopher who believed in the transmigration of souls

**hanged** (predatory animals could be tried and executed until the late seventeenth century)

**fell** cruel

**fleet** flit

**unhallowed dam** unholy mother

**starved** deadly

**rail** declaim abusively

**but offend'st** only does harm

**in loving visitation** on a friendly visit

**Balthazar** Portia has adopted the name of her servant at III.4.45, whom she sent to her cousin Dr Bellario to collect 'notes and garments'. By a dramatic coincidence, the Duke too consults Bellario of Padua; but the Duke is not aware of Portia's plot

**let him lack** deprive him of

**whose trial ... commendation** the test you make of him will recommend him better than my words

**Which is the merchant ...?** this question is standard court procedure. The judge requires the principals to identify themselves

**impugn** disallow

**danger** power

**The quality ... strained** the nature of mercy is such that it is not constrained or compelled

**It blesseth** cf. Acts 20:35 'It is more blessed to give than to receive'

**none of us Should see salvation** cf. Psalm 102:10–11, part of morning prayer: 'He hath not dealt with us after our sins, nor rewarded us according to our iniquities. For as high as the heaven is above the earth, so great is his mercy toward them that fear him'

**that same prayer** the Lord's Prayer ('Forgive us our trespasses, as we forgive them that trespass against us')

**mitigate** make more gentle

**My deeds ... head!** cf. Matthew 27:25

**bears down** overthrows

**power in Venice ... establishèd** Venice's respect for her own laws was legendary

**precedent** the chief rule of English common law

**Daniel** Shylock compares Portia to Daniel, the young judge who in the biblical story of Susannah and the Elders (Daniel 13) detects the fraud of the elders and prevents injustice. In the Bible Daniel is also called Baltassar

**thrice** Portia increases this from Bassanio's 'twice'; but in line 208 he less clearly offers 'ten times'

**oath** presumably in the synagogue in Act III Scene 1

**tenour** wording

**stay** take my stand

**Hath full relation** fully authorises

**balance** a variant plural form. The scales are a symbol of justice; the knife, of sacrifice

**armed** fortified in mind

**still** ever

**Repent but you** regret only

**with all my heart** willingly. To make a jest on the point of death shows the Renaissance gentleman's ability to make light of things, known as *sprezzatura*

**Barabbas** (stressed on the first syllable) the name of the thief whom the Jewish mob released instead of Jesus; the name also of Marlowe's Jew of Malta; and of a thief in Shakespeare's *Measure for Measure*

**Soft** wait

**scruple** an apothecary's weight; one-twentieth of a scruple is one grain

**merely** purely

**I'll stay ... question** I'll remain no longer to argue the case. Shylock tries to leave

**privy coffer** personal treasury

**'gainst all other voice** without appeal

**Down** kneel

**our** royal plural; also Christian

**Which humbleness ...** which asking pardon will reduce to a fine

**quit** remit

**in use** to administer in trust

**Two things ... more** with two further conditions

**presently** immediately

**possessed** possessed of

**son** son-in-law

**I am content** I accept the terms

**ten more** this would make up the twelve members of a jury – to convict him of murder

**gratify** reward

**cope** give in recompense for

**know me** (pun) recognise me / consider this an introduction / (to Bassanio) treat me as a wife

**hold out enemy** remain an enemy

SCENE 2    **Venice: The wives regain their rings**

Gratiano gives Bassanio's ring to Portia. Nerissa resolves to get back the ring she had given to Gratiano.

> **you are well o'ertane** I'm glad to have overtaken you
> **more advice** thinking further
> **my youth** i.e., Nerissa
> **old** plenty of
> **where I will tarry** the place where I'll await you

# ACT V

## SCENE 1    Belmont: All is put right

After Jessica and Lorenzo's duet, the arrival of Portia and Nerissa is announced; music greets them. When they return, the husbands are upbraided for giving the rings away. All are reconciled after Antonio swears upon his soul that Bassanio will never again break faith, and the ladies restore the rings. A letter tells that three of Antonio's ships are come to harbour. Lorenzo and Jessica learn of Shylock's will. The three couples go off.

'The moon shines bright' is the keynote of an exchange between Lorenzo and Jessica which adds nothing to plot but transforms the mood. See Textual Analysis, Text 3.

Formally the lovers' exchange is in marked contrast with everything in the play so far, except the song before Bassanio chooses the leaden casket. It is like an operatic duet about the beauty of the moonlit night as a setting for love. The lovers almost sing the names of the most famous lovers in literature.

High artifice is interrupted by an announcement, and Lancelot brings them down to earth, but Lorenzo returns us to moonlight, the heavens, and the music of the spheres. Music plays. The heroine enters and adds a final poetic aria.

This dose of romantic magic allows the mock-crisis of the broken promises and the revelation of identity to lead to the proper conclusion to both the romance and the comedy. This night is their wedding night.

Antonio, the Merchant, is (magically) restored to fortune, and his pledge of his soul for Bassanio's future fidelity plays a part in the final reconciliation.

**Troilus** Trojan prince parted from his love Cressida: a scene from Book 5 of Chaucer's *Troilus and Criseyde*

**Thisbe** lover of Pyramus in Chaucer's *Legend of Good Women*; frightened by a **lion**, she failed to make her rendezvous with Pyramus (a scene played in *A Midsummer Night's Dream*)

**Dido** lover of Aeneas, who left her at Carthage to found Rome; the **willow** is symbolic of deserted love; also from Chaucer's *Legend*

**waft** waved, beckoned

**Medea** witch who helped Jason to win the Golden Fleece (Act I.1.169 and III.2.240), also in the *Legend*; but her rejuvenation of Jason's father **Aeson** is from Ovid's *Metamorphoses*

**steal** creep away

**unthrift** thriftless, prodigal

**Stealing** (pun) enticing / saving

**shrew** sharp-tongued woman

**outnight** outdo in nocturnal comparisons

**holy crosses** wayside crosses

**hermit** (this is a fictional cover story)

**Sola** hunting cry

**Wo ha, ho** a falconer's call

**post** courier

**horn** carried by couriers, but here a horn of plenty also

**expect** await

**no matter** not so (emphatic)

**your music** your musicians

**Become** befit

**touches** strains

**patens** small golden dishes, used for the host at Holy Communion

**orb** star

**his motion** its orbit

**Still choiring** always singing together

**young-eyed cherubins** junior angels with piercing sight

**immortal souls** (human as well as angelic)

**this muddy ... decay** this earthly body

**Doth grossly close it** the soul. In the geocentric cosmos inherited from the Greeks, each planet is set in a crystal sphere guided by an order of angels, each sphere giving a musical note as it revolves. The cosmos makes a harmony which our immortal souls cannot hear. The stars have a fixed sphere which forms the floor of heaven

**Diana** the moon (who 'sleeps with Endymion' line 108)

**race** herd

**unhandled** unbroken

**mutual** common

**the poet** Ovid in *Metamorphoses*

**Orpheus** the first poet

**stockish** blockish (the trees)

**full of rage** enraged (the floods)

**his** its

**spoils** plunder. The line applies to Shylock, who at II.5.29 dislikes the 'vile squealing' of the fife

**Erebus** in classical legend, the dark region between earth and the underworld

**naughty** wicked

**music** musicians

**without respect** without context and relationship

**attended** expected

**Peace, ho!** cease your music

**speed** prosper

**take No note** make no remark

*tucket* flourish on a trumpet

**his trumpet** only noblemen had tuckets, and each was unique; Bassanio is Lord of Belmont

**We should hold ... sun** your presence turns our night into day, so that we have our day when they do on the other side of the globe

**be light** behave wantonly

**But God sort all!** let all be as God shall dispose

**in all sense** in reason

**acquitted of** requited for

**breathing courtesy** courteous language

**By yonder moon** an inconstant thing to swear by

**gelt** gelded

**poesy** motto inscribed on the inside of the ring

**cutler's poetry** a knife-maker's motto

**respective** regardful

**and if** if

**scrubbèd** shrub-like (in height)

**And 'twere to me** if it were to me

**virtue** special quality

**ceremony** sacred symbol

**held up** preserved

**candles of the night** stars

**liberal** free

**Lie not ... home** sleep not one night away from home

**Argus** the hundred-eyed watchman of classical legend

**be well advised** beware

**pen** (pun) pen / penis

**of credit** worthy of belief (a sarcasm)

**upon the forfeit** be the penalty

**advisedly** knowingly

**the mending ... In summer** i.e. remedying something which has not gone wrong

**amazed** bewildered

**Unseal this letter** (a theatrical miracle; and Portia miraculously knows its contents)

**life and living** cf. Shylock at IV.1.371–2

**road** anchorage

**manna** food miraculously provided in the desert (Exodus 16:15)

**not satisfied Of** not yet heard all about

**charge us ... inter'gatories** require us to answer specific questions (Portia reverts to legal jargon)

**Nerissa's ring** a final bawdy joke from Gratiano, since 'ring' could mean 'vulva'

# PART THREE

# CRITICAL APPROACHES

## COMEDY AND CONVENTION

*The Merchant of Venice* is one of Shakespeare's sixteen comedies. Comedy is a special kind of play in which the audience would expect to find a certain kind of story, with certain conventions. Drama involves complication and resolution. If tragedy ends in the death of the hero, comedy ends with a restoration of social order, typically in marriage. Although 'comic' means funny, tending to laughter, **comedic** means obeying the conventions of comedy as a form or genre. The chief of these is a happy resolution, as suggested by the title of *All's Well That Ends Well*, which is, however, not a very funny play. The rule of comedy is that, however serious the confusion, all ends well. The Italian poet Dante (1265–1326) wrote a *Commedia*, a journey through hell to purgatory and up to heaven, which ends well, but does not make its reader laugh.

Although genre (kind, or form) mattered to Shakespeare, he never abided by the classical division of drama into strictly comic and strictly serious. His comedies came to include problems increasingly difficult to resolve, and to take them more seriously; in some 'problem comedies', such as *Measure for Measure*, the final marriages do not resolve the issues of the play. Early in *The Merchant* (I.1.50) mention is made of 'two-headed Janus', both merry and sad, an emblem of the merry and sad masks of comedy and tragedy, and a signal that mixed drama is to come. The play follows many comedic conventions: its setting is urban, its persons middle class, it uses prose; there is a clownish comic servant (Gobbo) and a jester (Gratiano); plot confusion arises from disguise and deception, disaster is avoided, complications are resolved, marriages conclude.

*The Merchant* also follows conventions from **romance**, a medieval form of story full of marvellous adventure, owing much to folk- and fairytale, in which love finds a way: 'Jack shall have Jill, And all shall be well'. In Roman comedy, grasping fathers tried to marry unwilling daughters to rich old men. Shakespeare's romantic comedy is less harsh and farcical than this, more gentle, make-believe and idealist; it uses verse; sometimes the young lovers – or the audience – learn something along the way. Other comedic conventions are a festive or party atmosphere, with a clown or fool and some use of song. *The Merchant* has all these elements, blended in a complex plot owing much to folktale (the flesh-bond) and fairytale (the princess and the caskets: see Literary Background, on Sources). Shakespeare emphasises comedic patterns by having three marriages, and raising the possibility of a fourth, between Lancelot and a Moorish girl whom he has made pregnant (III.5.30–35). In comedy, situation normally matters more than character, but Shylock's character is developed to such a point that when his wicked plot is foiled we do not laugh at him. Some Elizabethans will have laughed in The Theatre, as the angry Gratiano does. Gratiano would have hanged Shylock; but we are shown the relative clemency of the Duke and Antonio.

# THEMES

## LOVE, MARRIAGE AND FRIENDSHIP

In romantic comedy, love finds a way round all obstacles. In the literature of the Middle Ages, love gradually became a popular motive for marriage, in addition to the more practical reasons of procreation and keeping property in the family. Shakespeare's romantic comedies lead up to and end with marriages, including one noble marriage. The suitor loves and serves his lady; but after marriage the wife loves and serves the husband. As soon as Bassanio has chosen rightly, Portia calls him Lord: 'her Lord, her governor, her king' (III.2.165), adding 'Myself, and what is mine, to you and yours / Is now converted'. The husband's corresponding obligations are understood rather than expressed here; but the two are 'one flesh'. Portia behaves throughout as an ideal daughter and wife, according to the ideals of the day.

A letter now arrives announcing Antonio's ruin. Bassanio tells Portia, 'I have engaged myself to a dear friend' (II.2.260). Portia offers her fortune: what was hers is his; and what is his is Antonio's. The wedding takes place offstage. The Renaissance ideal of noble friendship between men is less familiar today than the ideal of marriage. Lorenzo praises Portia's 'noble and true conceit / Of god-like amity' (III.4.2–3).

Ideal male friendship is a theme of Renaissance writing; it is called Platonic because first found in the *Phaedrus* of Plato, the Greek philosopher of the fifth century BC whose works were revived at the Renaissance. Noble male friendship would be known to the educated from Castiglione's *Book of the Courtier* (1528), translated into English by Sir Thomas Hoby (1561). In the Renaissance idea, this love assumed no active sexual origin or outcome, and was quite compatible with marriage. In Shakespeare's *Sonnets* the older man encourages the younger to marry. Antonio's unconditional love for Bassanio is of this kind, and may owe something to *Il Pecorone*, in which he is the young man's adopted father (see Literary Background, on Sources). Bassanio is introduced to us as Antonio's 'most noble kinsman', a term which could be used for a godson. In Shakespeare's early play, *Love's Labour's Lost*, he shows how a Platonic Academy based on male friendship breaks down because it underestimates men's need for women; Shakespeare also collaborated in a play with the title *Two Noble Kinsmen*. It is remarkable that neither Portia nor Antonio show any jealousy of the other's love for Bassanio, although Antonio's sadness remains.

# MONEY

Money is a theme of the love plot as well as the hate plot of *The Merchant*. Bassanio's need for money to pay court to Portia, 'a lady richly left', is what puts Antonio in the power of Shylock. Antonio and Shylock are very different merchants, yet all merchants try to make money. And Jessica brings plenty of money with her when she elopes with Lorenzo: she throws down a casket. She then spends extravagantly the money her father had won so carefully. Attitudes to the getting and spending of money are a theme of the play. Wealth does not make Portia happy; she needs to love and be loved. Spending money is more fun than getting it, and generosity is better than meanness. Yet generosity is not the word for a daughter exchanging a turquoise ring for a monkey. Life with Shylock must have been grim, but the ring Jessica steals and then exchanges for a monkey was the ring her mother gave to her father. If Bassanio has been extravagant, Jessica is prodigal; unlike the Prodigal Son, she does not go back to her father for forgiveness. Is the implication that she has nothing to be ashamed of?

The Elizabethan nobility and gentry needed money to keep up the generosity expected of their rank, but rents from land could not keep up with rampant inflation, still less with the wealth made in the City of

London. Gentlemen like Sir Philip Sidney and aristocrats like the Earl of Essex owed huge sums to City merchants – a common topic in Elizabethan writing. Thomas Nashe wrote that 'The usurer eateth up the gentleman, and the gentleman the yeoman, and all three being devoured one of another, do nothing but complain.' The old social hierarchy was under violent strain. Commerce was almost respectable, and moneylending almost acceptable; yet the taking of interest was unpopular and usury, although legal, was still widely regarded as morally wrong (see Historical Background, on Usury). The new merchant venturers, however, who financed international trade as Antonio does, had a certain glamour.

Venice (see Historical Background, on Venice) was a mercantile city, and its luxurious life is based not on land and title but on commerce, law and credit. Although Bassanio has been a prodigal son (or godson), his godfather forgives him and is happy to finance his adventure or 'pilgrimage' to Belmont. Bassanio deserves Portia because he is not taken in by 'outward shows', the glamour of precious metals; he is granted a moral insight. But Jessica's unfilial theft of her father's gold raises questions. Does her love-scene with Lorenzo in Act V Scene 1 redeem their love? Such a transformation of character could be an **allegory** of the effect of conversion and of marriage. It is also convenient for dramatic purpose, effacing the trial scene and providing romance for the reunion of Portia and Bassanio.

Portia's wealth is fabulous: she is the Golden Fleece won by Jason, and Belmont is an Eldorado of which Bassanio becomes lord. But Portia's readiness to give her fortune and herself away for love is matched by Antonio's. This loving and giving is in stark contrast to a greed which prefers ducats to a daughter and a hate which prefers a pound of flesh to thousands of ducats. Royal merchants are generous. Yet the association of wealth with glamour and alluring appearance raises questions in the scene of Jessica's elopement. She cheats her father, as Portia does not. Shakespeare parallels these daughters who marry adventurers of various degrees of merit, and he parallels their engagements. When the joker Gratiano has won Nerissa, he says to Bassanio that 'we are the Jasons'; but he is not Bassanio, and his conduct in the trial scene is neither heroic, gentle nor Christian. Parallelism and silent comparison are favourite techniques of this playwright. Gold rings are tokens of exchange, of wealth, and of engagement; it is worth comparing the fates of the rings belonging to Leah, Nerissa and Portia.

## JUSTICE AND MERCY

The keynote of the play is Portia's 'The quality of mercy is not strained', in the trial scene. It alerts the audience to what is at issue. Shylock has the right in law to his pound of flesh, and refuses the plea for mercy. He insists on justice, the law, his bond. Portia likewise refuses Bassanio's plea that she should relax the law, knowing that in the exact wording of the bond lies Antonio's salvation. Although every argument and move counts in this trial scene, the trial is dramatic rather than legal. Drama is conflict, and the trial is a contest between two radically opposed attitudes to the human life which is at stake.

Portia's argument for mercy is the Christian one that no-one deserves salvation, for it is only God's mercy that can save a human soul. It does not move Shylock, who demands justice according to the law. Yet Shylock's true motive is not respect for law, but revenge. Jessica says that she has heard him swear to his Jewish friends 'That he would rather have Antonio's flesh / Than twenty times the value of the sum / That he did owe him' (III.2.285–7). On first seeing Antonio, Shylock's first lines are

How like a fawning publican he looks.
I hate him for he is a Christian. (I.3.33–4)

A Christian audience would identify Shylock's attitude here as that of the righteous Pharisee proud of his religious observance who scorns the humble publican who knows he is a sinner (Luke 18:9–14). Jews were seen by Christians as Pharisees, observers of the old law of Moses, rather than of the new law that Jesus gave, of love for God and of neighbour, and of forgiveness and turning the other cheek. The Gospels often show the Pharisees trying to catch Jesus breaking the letter of the law: as when he declines to condemn the woman taken in adultery. St Paul also contrasts the Old Law (the Mosaic law) with the New Law of love.

Such a Christian view of Judaism is, however, partial and unfair, for the Jews of the Old Testament relied on the mercy of God, especially in the Psalms, the prayerbook of Jews before it was that of Christians: 'If thou, Lord, shouldest mark us according to our iniquities, O Lord, who shall stand?' (Psalm 130). But Shylock's early speeches are full of the Patriarchs Abraham and Jacob, and of the Law; he speaks of Jews as 'my tribe'. He seems a stiff, tribal and primitive Jew, and does not quote the spiritual wisdom of the Psalms or the Prophets. This would confirm the hostile stereotype, prevalent in Shakespeare's day, of Jews as a separate people, harsh and retaliatory. Shylock's insistence on blood contrasts with Antonio's willingness to lay down his life for his friend, a version of the supreme Christian ideal of love. Antonio forgives Bassanio's prodigality; Shylock cannot forgive Jessica's. The play's fifth act shows women forgiving men for having broken their word and given away their rings, a forgiveness which leads to the reconciliation required by comedy.

Two figures are left out of the reconciliation, Shylock and Antonio. The self-sacrificing Antonio is left alone, with the token consolation of three ships miraculously restored. Shylock's position is discussed in Characterisation below, together with the question of the justice of his punishment.

## CHARACTERISATION

The *Merchant* has four leading characters – Antonio, Bassanio, Portia and Shylock – with several minor characters. It should be remembered that although Shakespeare deepens his major characters and gives them a psychology, drama does not allow the fullness of all-round depiction and exploration found in some novels. We learn much of the thoughts of Hamlet and other tragic characters, but less of characters in comedy.

### ANTONIO

Antonio is 'sad' and unselfish. His noble friendship for his kinsman Bassanio is such that 'He only loves the world for him' (II.8.51). Antonio is a 'royal merchant' with ships trading to the Levant, England and Mexico: 'argosies with portly sail / Like signors and rich burghers of the flood.' The glamour of ships is established by such awestruck comments, but so are the perils of the sea: we hear of spices scattered on the stream and of roaring waters enrobed with silk. Antonio is patient with Bassanio's extravagance and readily agrees to lend him more. His sadness may be a sign of suffering to come.

Shylock declares hatred for Antonio yet addresses him deferentially. Antonio is open about his distaste for Shylock: he breaks a custom in borrowing money at interest; he has rescued those who owed Shylock interest and could not pay. (For the ensuing argument about usury, see Historical Background, on Usury). He admits calling Shylock a misbeliever and a cut-throat dog and spitting on him; he says he would do so again. In his anger, he is surprised by Shylock's offer of friendship, and an interest-free loan; and risks the fantastic penalty of a pound of flesh. Bassanio is suspicious, but Antonio takes the bait, as the plot requires.

In later scenes Antonio is gentle, patient and unselfish. He conceals his sorrow at Bassanio's departure for Belmont, wishing him success. He faces the trial with resignation: 'I am a tainted wether of the flock'. This may be a cue as to how the audience should see him rather than a revelation of character. He is ready to face death if he can say goodbye to Bassanio. He urges the sending of the ring after Portia. He takes the blame for the quarrel between the lovers in Act V and pledges his soul that Bassanio will be true. He passes the ring to Bassanio; he is left alone at the end.

His treatment of Shylock needs examination; he asks the Duke to let Shylock off the state's share and declines to takes his half of Shylock's estate except as a trustee for Jessica and Lorenzo. This is consistent with his principle that he does not profit from the misfortunes of others. His conditions are that Shylock leaves his estate to his daughter and becomes a Christian, or his estate is forfeit.

Difficulties in Antonio's character arise from historical changes in values. In the absence of the Renaissance ideal of noble friendship, Antonio's love for a man might seem homosexual. The demand that Shylock become a Christian denies liberty of religion. But in 1600 such a liberty was unknown, and Christian doctrine was that without conversion Shylock's soul would be damned. In the event, Shylock agrees to give up his religion rather than his living as a moneylender. It is hard to forget Antonio's insults to Shylock, for which he sees no need to apologise. Shylock may be a 'cut-throat' usurer, but he is not a dog and does not deserve to be spat at. We cannot condone Antonio's treatment, for it is a striking exception to his general courtesy and confirms the general rule that Christians in the play taunt Shylock in a way that shows no Christian humility. All this is, however, modified by the mercy shown by Antonio to a man who has tried to kill him.

# BASSANIO

Bassanio is a young gentleman, a 'noble kinsman' of Antonio's, and perhaps (as in the source, *Il Pecorone*) an adopted son, or a godson to the older man. He is embarrassed to ask his old friend Antonio for money, but not ashamed, though he has wasted money that Antonio had already advanced him. Aspiring to marry Portia, he needs money, as young gentlemen often do. The audience might be expected to be as indulgent as Antonio.

His theatrical role is that of the young male lead, stylish, enterprising, decent if not heroic. Youth is his leading characteristic: he is impulsive, gallant, generous but slightly immature. He is not a good credit risk: his policy of firing a second arrow to find a first he has lost might not impress a bank manager. But he ventures for Portia, and, at the crucial test, chooses rightly: his instincts are good. He had had the sense to suspect Shylock's 'merry sport': 'I like not fair terms and a villain's mind.' Compared with the noisy Gratiano, whom he more than generously allows to come with him to Belmont, he is gentle, even noble. His reactions to Antonio's letter and at the trial are heartfelt; he offers his life (evoking a witty response from Portia), but can do nothing. As Portia's husband, he cannot reciprocate his friend's love, although he defers to Antonio's sense of obligation and gives away Portia's ring. Is he right to do so? He has less presence of mind than his wife. Does that matter? He is the least of the four main players.

# PORTIA

Portia's role is that of golden princess, prize and bride in the fairytale casket test; Shakespeare fills Belmont with glamour, wealth, exotic visitors, music and moonlight. He changes the lady of his source from a sexual temptress to a young woman, magical but distinctly human. When she reviews her suitors with Nerissa, she is not just a beautiful and dutiful daughter, but a girl of independent mind, bored, not easily pleased, with a witty tongue, a shrewd judgement and a heart vulnerable to love. She is ceremonious to her grand suitors, yet relieved when they fail. Before Bassanio chooses, she is highly excited and emotional, yet resists the temptation to guide his choice. When his friend's plight is known, she is generous, quick, decisive: he must go to his friend but marry first. She keeps quiet about her rescue attempt. From passive heroine she becomes active hero. Her performance in the trial (a gift to boy actor and to actress) is masterly, first setting out rights and wrongs ('The quality of mercy is not strained'), then leading Shylock into the written trap in which he had caught Antonio. Her skill and touch are no less sure after the trial, as she rapidly manipulates her 'merry sport' in Venice and at Belmont. She has the gifts of an actor-manager, getting the most out of each situation. It seems that Shakespeare has succeeded in the impossible task of making a young, beautiful, clever and rich woman into a virtuous example of selfless love, while persuading us that she is hard-headed, modest, witty and good fun.

## SHYLOCK

Shylock appears in five scenes and speaks less than Bassanio or Portia, yet he dominates, even on the page. The traits of his character are rapidly laid down and repeated: focus on money, hatred of Christians, pride in Jewish identity, caution, calculation, cunning, experience, inflexible will (see Textual Analysis, Text 1). Our attitude to Shylock varies sharply. We recoil from his expressed hatred, but when we hear of his treatment by Antonio, we sympathise. He makes Antonio angry, then surprises him with an offer of friendship and an interest-free loan; this has a 'merry' clause, but Antonio takes the bait. We see Shylock's skill as a negotiator; then, his close-fistedness with his servant and possessiveness towards his daughter reveal him as a domestic tyrant. But when Jessica elopes, scattering money and family jewels, we see him taunted by Christians and tortured by Tubal's news. His emotion is intense, and his pain evokes pity, followed by revulsion: for his money-lust is such that he would rather have his daughter lying at his feet, dead, with the money in the coffin and the jewel in her ear: he prefer his ducats to his daughter, as the boys in Venice say. It is a defining moment: disgust kills the sympathy aroused by 'If you prick us, do we not bleed?' and prepares us for its conclusion: 'If you wrong us, shall we not revenge?' This bloody revenge puts Shylock beyond what Christianity can approve.

His performance at the trial is dominating, unbending, obsessive: he savours the prospect of revenge, exposes the hypocrisy of Christian slave-holding, and dismisses with contempt all pleas for mercy and offers of money. He meets his match in Portia, and when he is surprised, outwitted and prevented from taking his revenge, the audience must have rejoiced. At the climax, with whetted knife raised and the scales waiting, the drama of the moment banishes considerations of character. Our feelings sway as we watch Shylock trying to save 9,000 ducats, then 3,000 ducats, then his dignity. He tries to leave, but must face the penalty for attempting the life of a citizen. He is told to kneel for mercy, and a kind of mercy is extended to him. He says he is 'content'. The different reactions of Portia, Gratiano, the Duke and Antonio cause us to think about justice rather than character, and we shall not all come to the same conclusions. Shylock leaves quickly, unwell, and we are soon made to think of other things: tricks, disguises, moonlight, music and the renewal of love. But Shylock's fierce emotions trouble the memory as we think over the justice of his fate. Comedies with happy endings can be serious.

Shylock, like Portia, is a character taken from an old story and much changed by Shakespeare. The primitive stage Jew of tradition, a comic villain, is given human feelings and pride of family, unlike Marlowe's Jew of Malta. This Jew is no longer a caricature, though he remains the villain of a story where evil is not all on one side. Some of the disagreements over Shylock are due to the **paradox** that he is both the devilish, bloodthirsty wolf that Gratiano thinks him and also the human victim of snubs and vilification which make his revenge understandable: 'The villainy you teach me I will execute.' Most of the disagreements over Shylock come from long-term changes in attitudes since 1600 (see Critical History). These changes began at the time of Shakespeare.

## MINOR CHARACTERS

Characters in plays, and particularly minor characters, sometimes change their roles and their natures to meet the demands of the theatre and of the plot. The most interesting of the many lesser characters in *The Merchant* are Gratiano, Lancelot Gobbo, Lorenzo and Jessica. GRATIANO 'plays the Fool' (I.1.79) to Antonio's young friends: he is a mocker, a noisy talker, a gentleman-clown. His role is partly derived from the comic Vice of the Morality Plays, the tempter-entertainer. As Bassanio's second, he wins Portia's lady-in-waiting Nerissa (boasting 'We are the Jasons') and loses the ring she gives him. At the trial, he baits Shylock and demands vengeance. Gratiano is often a foil to deeper characters, bringing out by contrast Antonio's sadness, Bassanio's discretion, and the mercy of the nobler

Venetians. He has the last word, a bawdy joke. On the other hand, his moral critique of affected gravity is reasonable (though Antonio's sadness is real, not affected), and his 'How like a younger or a prodigal' (II.6.15) is a key speech of the play.

The stage-direction for LANCELOT GOBBO on his first appearance reads 'Enter Clown'. With his comic Anglo-Italian name, his role is a traditional one, written for the company's professional comedian, Will Kemp. In accordance with **comic** tradition, he makes cruel fun of his father. Lancelot is an unedifying comic servant whose prose makes us laugh; a 'wit-snapper' whose comic patter (now rather obscure) includes plays on words, catch-phrases, rude jokes (known as 'bawdy'), **malapropism** and nonsense. He lightens the mood and offsets the tragic potentiality of the plot, although at times he is shrewd. He jokingly admits (in III.5) that he has got a black girl pregnant; but this issue is not followed up in the play.

The lovers LORENZO and JESSICA seem to change their natures after they run away together. At Belmont they are romantic lovers (see Textual Analysis: Text 3), but earlier their elopement raises some doubts. When Jessica dares to escape from her father's house of bondage, we sympathise, even when she throws down a 'casket' of his money to Lorenzo, who then praises her as 'wise, fair and true' (II.6.57). Yet on their honeymoon spree, Jessica is rumoured to have given a turquoise in exchange for a monkey. What her father had treasured, she squanders. Lorenzo marries for love *and* money, as does Bassanio; a casket is again involved. Jessica also becomes a Christian, a Gentile, a *gentle* (noble) Venetian. The questions raised by such a conversion are reabsorbed into the comic onrush of the play; but the case of Jessica confirms that the role of minor characters is often to cast light on the themes of the play and the values of others.

## STYLE AND LANGUAGE

### VERSE DRAMA: PROSE AND POETRY

Like other poetic dramatists of his day, Shakespeare used prose as well as verse. Society was hierarchical, and as the Renaissance theory of **decorum** or form prescribed, high style dignified kings and tragedy, low style was used for servants and comedy. Shakespeare and his audience shared a sense of linguistic **register** (high, middle and low areas of the vocabulary). *The Merchant* uses prose for servants, clowns, chat, jokes, realism and comedy; verse for courtiers, ideals and romance. In *The Merchant*, financial terms and quayside gossip are in 'low' prose, whereas the trial is in verse, and courtship in a 'high' formal poetry which is almost music.

Verse and music are based on measures of time, unlike prose. Verse is measured prose; song is verse put to music. Modern films, plays and television drama are in prose, and although prose has more than one register, these modern media have other resources. Shakespeare's stage had no scenery or lighting, and he needed the extra resources of verse. Poetic drama is like opera: narrative passages have little or no music; big scenes need more music; the best tunes are reserved for dramatic duets and emotional arias.

Prose and verse intensify contrast when the same thing is shown at different levels. Thus, after Shylock has told in verse how Jacob, helped by his wise mother, fooled his blind father into giving him something which was not his due, we see Lancelot Gobbo getting his blind father to help him get a new position; the comic version is in prose. This parallel might recall a more distant parallel: the prodigal Bassanio getting a loan from a god-father, who is (in worldly terms) blinded by his love for him. Another contrast is that Bassanio asks Antonio for help in verse, while Shylock curses his prodigal daughter in prose. Much of the variety of *The Merchant* comes from the range of stylistic resources at Shakespeare's command. This enables him, after the drama of Shylock's exit, to turn on the maximum poetic power in the loving exchanges between Lorenzo and Jessica in order to recreate the magic of Belmont so that the play can end with the renewal of love.

L ANGUAGE, IMAGERY AND THEME

Poetry was once defined by the American poet Ezra Pound as 'bee-yewtiful thoughts in flowery langwidge'. Pound was mocking the monotony of post-Romantic poetry. In this 'bee-yewtiful' sense, Shakespeare was not a poetic dramatist but a language dramatist. He made plays out of all kinds of language. On the stage, Romantic poetry is not often called for, even in romantic comedy. The most telling images in *The Merchant* are shocking thoughts in brutal language: Shylock's 'I would my daughter were dead at my foot, and the jewels in her ear,' or his comparison of Antonio to a rat to be poisoned. Some key images of the play are simply phrases which raise questions: 'a royal merchant'; 'a pound of flesh'. Thus language is hard to separate from theme. A writer is looking for the right word, not the beautiful word.

### LANGUAGE AND CHARACTER-CREATION

Shakespeare opens scenes with words which create character and theme at once. Antonio begins Act I Scene 1: 'In sooth, I know not why I am so sad'. Portia begins Scene 2: 'By my troth, Nerissa, my little body is aweary of this great world.' Shylock opens Scene 3 with 'Three thousand ducats, well', establishing situation as well as character and theme. Lorenzo's first words to Jessica in Act 2 Scene 4 tell us his plan *and* that he is ashamed of it: 'Nay, we will slink away in supper time.' Shylock's calculating repetition of words suggests that to him a word may be a term in a contract (see Textual Analysis, Text 1). A sense of his different ethnic identity is created early by his speech habits: he speaks of 'our tribe' (Jews); he will not 'eat with you' (Christians). He constantly uses Hebrew names: Jacob, Abraham, Hagar and Leah. His idioms and references are different – either proudly patriarchal, or grossly physical. He speaks of things: jewels, money, sheep, cats, rats, pigs, blood, urine, flesh. The Christians in turn call him a dog, spurn him with their feet, spit on him. To them he is a cur, a wolf, a devil, subhuman. He replies by reminding them of the physical basis of their common humanity: 'If you prick us, do we not bleed?' In return, he wants blood.

### SPECIAL LANGUAGE AND ANALOGY

Shylock has his own prose, and uses special Jewish vocabulary which marks him as different. Other special forms of language in the play are Christian and classical. These would not in themselves have seemed special to Shakespeare's audience; educated men read Latin, and everyone went to church on Sunday. It was a Christian society familiar with the Bible from readings at church, and from private reading. The poet whom Shakespeare most often quotes and imitates, however, is the pagan Ovid: his *Metamorphoses*, as a guide to mythology, and his legends of classical lovers. The play is full of analogies or parallels to Christian and classical stories.

## CLASSICAL ANALOGIES

These are used for two aspects of the casket plot: Bassanio's adventure to Belmont, and the lavish Ovidian imagery of love scenes, notably the Casket scene and the duet in Act V Scene 1 between Lorenzo and Jessica (discussed in Textual Analysis, Text 3). Bassanio likens Portia's 'sunny locks' to the Golden Fleece sought by Jason and his Argonauts, guarded by a dragon. Jason won the Fleece with the help of the magic of Medea, and there is something magic about Belmont and its 'Lady richly left'. She laughingly likens Bassanio to Alcides (Hercules in Latin), a hero who performed labours such as rescuing a virgin from a sea-monster. Choosing a casket is a test of discrimination rather than of courage, though much depends upon it. When Bassanio has done so, Gratiano claims that 'we are the Jasons, we have won the Fleece'; rather like a Grand Prix winner spraying champagne. But is their adventure heroic, or fortunate (and fortune-bringing)? How does its heroism compare with Portia's rescue of Antonio? Is the hero of the play Balthazar?

## CHRISTIAN LANGUAGE

There is more Christian language in *The Merchant* than in any other comedy, partly because of its story of the Jew and the flesh-bond. Shakespeare used Genesis to create an Old Testament religious identity for Shylock; he did not want to leave him as a villain whom we could laugh at when baulked of his prey. He also makes Shylock pointedly anti-Christian: he mocks the New Testament, with his insulting references to the Nazarite, the Gadarene swine and the publican (see Textual Analysis, Text 1). He wishes that 'any of the stock of Barabbas' had been Jessica's husband rather than a Christian: Barabbas was the thief whom the Jewish mob released, preferring to crucify Jesus. What effect would Shylock's gibes have upon the audience?

The parable of the Prodigal Son is an evident analogy to the wasteful Bassanio returning to his forgiving (god)father. It is recalled again in the image of the strumpet wind (II.6.15). Forgiveness is a theme of the play (see Justice and Mercy), and so is sacrifice. Some critics see Antonio's willingness to die for Bassanio as a parallel with Christ's willingness to offer himself as the victim at the Paschal feast, taking the sins of mankind upon him, like the scapegoat of the Old Testament. Such parallels between religion and contemporary life were commonplace in drama. But the parallel is partial: Antonio's blood is not spilt, though he offers his soul to reconcile Portia and his beloved Bassanio. A negative parallel is more likely: that we are to see in Shylock's knife and scales a reminder of the blood-sacrifice, as against the advice freely to forgive those who trespass against us, given in Portia's 'The quality of mercy is not strained'.

## WORD PLAY

There are many other kinds of language in *The Merchant*, including Lancelot's nonsense and **malapropism**. But, as often in Shakespeare, there is sense inside some of the nonsense. Shakespeare had a weakness for puns, sometimes known as quibbles. Dr Johnson said that 'A quibble was to Shakespeare the fatal Cleopatra for which he lost the world and was content to lose it.' Johnson thought a pun a low form of humour, and that a cheap pun sacrificed all seriousness. But Shakespeare's idea of **decorum** was much less rigid; he often makes a serious point with a weak play on words. Indeed he plays on the last word in the play.

# PART FOUR

# Textual analysis

The analysis of extract 1 concentrates chiefly on character, of extract 2 on theme, and of extract 3 on poetic language.

## TEXT 1   INTRODUCING SHYLOCK

*Enter* BASSANIO *with* SHYLOCK *the Jew*

SHYLOCK: Three thousand ducats, well.

BASSANIO: Ay, sir, for three months.

SHYLOCK: For three months, well.

BASSANIO: For the which, as I told you, Antonio shall be bound.

SHYLOCK: Antonio shall become bound, well.

BASSANIO: May you stead me? Will you pleasure me? Shall I know your answer?

SHYLOCK: Three thousand ducats for three months, and Antonio bound.

BASSANIO: Your answer to that?

SHYLOCK: Antonio is a good man –

BASSANIO: Have you heard any imputation to the contrary?

SHYLOCK: Ho no, no, no, no: my meaning in saying he is a good man is to have you understand me that he is sufficient. Yet his means are in supposition: he hath an argosy bound to Tripolis, another to the Indies; I understand moreover upon the Rialto he hath a third at Mexico, a fourth for England, and other ventures he hath squandered abroad. But ships are but boards, sailors but men; there be land rats, and water rats, water thieves and land thieves – I mean pirates – and then there is the peril of waters, winds and rocks. The man is notwithstanding sufficient. Three thousand ducats; I think I may take his bond.

BASSANIO: Be assured you may.

SHYLOCK: I will be assured I may; and that I may be assured, I will bethink me – may I speak with Antonio?

BASSANIO: If it please you to dine with us –

SHYLOCK: Yes, to smell pork, to eat of the habitation which your prophet the Nazarite conjured the devil into. I will buy with you, sell with you, talk with you, walk with you, and so following; but I will not eat with you, drink with you, nor pray with you. What news on the Rialto? Who is he comes here?

*Enter* ANTONIO

BASSANIO: This is Signor Antonio.

SHYLOCK: [*Aside*] How like a fawning publican he looks!
I hate him for he is a Christian; But more, for that in low simplicity
He lends out money gratis, and brings down
The rate of usance here with us in Venice.
If I can catch him once upon the hip,
I will feed fat the ancient grudge I bear him.
He hates our sacred nation, and he rails
Even there where merchants most do congregate
On me, my bargains, and my well-won thrift
Which he calls interest. Cursèd be my tribe
If I forgive him!

BASSANIO:          Shylock, do you hear?

SHYLOCK: I am debating of my present store ... (I.3.1–42)

The function of the scene is, first, **exposition** of the terms of the bond, and then of the antipathy between Jew and Christian. Language and dialogue establish Shylock's character, and the theme of forgiveness. Stage by stage, Shylock's nature is dramatically revealed.

In the opening exchange as Shylock and Bassanio walk on (lines 1–29), terms are repeated, and characters contrasted: old businessman and noble young client. Repetition gets the terms into our heads. Shylock is wary, Bassanio wordy (as with Antonio in Act I Scene 1). The repetition of 'three' is echoed in Bassanio's triple question (lines 5–6). Shylock repeats the terms in a formula rather than answering yes or no. He plays cat and mouse: when Bassanio presses his question, Shylock turns to discussing Antonio. He seems unwilling; only later do we learn that he is excited at this chance to catch Antonio. Although quiet and simple, the opening creates curiosity and suspense.

In a longer speech at line 12 he considers Antonio as a business proposition: he is 'good' (= 'sufficient'), even if his money is all at sea: 'I *may* take his bond'. Bassanio presses; Shylock asks to see Antonio, Bassanio asks him to dinner, Shylock refuses. Caution gives way to passion with: 'Yes, to smell pork.' This sardonic outburst associates Jesus with pork, the smell of which is offensive to Orthodox Jews. In the Old Testament, pigs are prohibited to Jews as 'unclean' animals: not only inedible, but also unfit for ritual sacrifice because they divide the hoof, admitting excrement into contact with their flesh; they are unfit for God or man. Jesus of Nazareth is 'your prophet' not, as Christians believe, the Son of God. Thus Shylock refuses the invitation with an insult. He lists with mounting anger what Jewish Law says he may and may not do: trade or talk with Gentiles, but not eat or pray with them. He gives physical expression to the revulsion he feels for Christians: smell and food express religion and race. He is revealed as a smouldering, passionate man. The different ways in which the moneylender and the gentleman look at things is also a theme: the glamorous 'argosies' of Act I Scene 1 are reduced to physical and financial risks: 'Ships are but boards.' (**Ironically**, he agrees in Act II to eat with Christians, and he finally prays *to* their Duke [IV.1.391].)

Shylock's **aside** (a remark unheard by others onstage) makes plain what before was implied (unless dress and manner have told us already that he is the villain). The aside is a convention by which the dramatist tells the audience of motives hidden from other characters. Shylock's revulsion at the sight of Antonio is expressed in the word 'publican', a tax-collector who took money from fellow Jews. 'I hate him for he is a Christian' makes clear, before Shylock meets Antonio, that he hates him on religious grounds, but *more* as a business enemy. As Shylock goes on, it is hard to tell whether he is more a usurer than a Jew. He wants to 'catch [Antonio] once *upon the hip*' (a biblical phrase, used against him later by Gratiano).

The 'ancient grudge' felt by 'our sacred nation' is identified with financial rivalry: Antonio's widely advertised contempt for 'our thrift / Which he calls interest' is matched by Shylock's commercial contempt for lending money 'gratis' (see Historical Background, on Usury). How would the audience react to the argument that Antonio's practice brings down the rate of usury that Jews can charge in Venice? The connection between religious/ethnic identity and the play's moral theme is summed up in 'Cursèd be my tribe / If I forgive him!'

At this point we know that Shylock hates Christians and has formed a malicious plan to 'catch' Antonio, before he meets him; he will not forgive. His more personal motive for hating Antonio appears later in this scene. He first appears as different, cautious; then as one who takes and gives offence; and finally as consumed with revenge.

His ill-feeling comes out in a prose tirade to Bassanio; the sight of Antonio brings a passionate verse declaration. Antonio does not acknowledge the Jew, who speaks openly to the audience, but not to his enemy.

## TEXT 2    THE TRIAL'S CONCLUSION

PORTIA: ... Down, therefore, and beg mercy of the Duke.

GRATIANO: Beg that thou mayst have leave to hang thyself –
And yet, thy wealth being forfeit to the state,
Thou hast not left the value of a cord;
Therefore thou must be hanged at the state's charge.

DUKE: That thou shalt see the difference of our spirit,
I pardon thee thy life before thou ask it.
For half thy wealth, it is Antonio's;
The other half comes to the general state,
Which humbleness may drive unto a fine.

PORTIA: Ay, for the state, not for Antonio.

SHYLOCK: Nay, take my life and all, pardon not that:
You take my house when you do take the prop
That doth sustain my house; you take my life
When you do take the means whereby I live.

PORTIA: What mercy can you render him, Antonio?

GRATIANO: A halter gratis – nothing else, for God's sake.

ANTONIO: So please my lord the Duke and all the court
To quit the fine for one half of his goods,
I am content, so he will let me have
The other half in use, to render it

Upon his death unto the gentleman
That lately stole his daughter.
Two things provided more: that for this favour
He presently become a Christian;
The other, that he do record a gift,
Here in the court, of all he dies possessed
Unto his son Lorenzo and his daughter.

DUKE: He shall do this, or else I do recant
The pardon that I late pronouncèd here.

PORTIA: Art thou contented, Jew? What dost thou say?

SHYLOCK: I am content.

PORTIA:                    Clerk, draw a deed of gift.

SHYLOCK: I pray you give me leave to go from hence;
I am not well. Send the deed after me
And I will sign it.
DUKE:                    Get thee gone, but do it.

GRATIANO: In christening shalt thou have two godfathers:
Had I been judge, thou shouldst have had ten more,
To bring thee to the gallows, not to the font.

*Exit* [*Shylock*]                        (IV.1.359–36)

This is the grand climax of the trial and of the play, focusing on the central conflict of justice and mercy. The pound of flesh has escaped Shylock, and he has just heard that the penalty for attempted murder is death and forfeit of goods. Portia ends with a command to beg for mercy. Does Shylock kneel?

Gratiano jokes that Shylock will have to beg for a rope to hang himself since he will have no money to buy one. A jester and cheerful loud-mouth before the trial, Gratiano is now a scoffer. His voice is that of a wise-cracking spectator at a mass sport (bear-baiting was popular at the time). What would its effect be on the original spectators in The Theatre? Would all react alike? Famous theatrical scoffers were the Jews and Romans who taunted Jesus at his trial and crucifixion in medieval Passion Plays. The trial here may be a reversal or **parody** of that ('parody': an imitation of the style of a well-known work, exaggerating its features for comic purposes). It is essential to understand the exact terms of what follows.

Ignoring Gratiano, the Duke pardons Shylock's life 'before thou ask it'. He points out that Christians forgive without being asked. This is an illustration not of the Duke's character, but of the play's theme: 'the quality of mercy' is that it is not 'strained' (= constrained, bound) but free, gratis. He repeats the financial penalties: half to the state, half to the intended victim. If Shylock is humble (and asks forgiveness like a Christian), the state's share will be reduced. Portia now puts the ball in Antonio's court.

Shylock's reaction to Christian mercy is indignant: he would rather not be pardoned; he would prefer death to losing his money, for his money is his living, his life. 'House' can mean family, tribe; also private or business house. There is spirit in his reaction, but what else does it reveal?

Ignoring Shylock's defiance, Portia asks Antonio if he can match the Duke's forgiveness. Gratiano repeats his hanging joke, bringing farce into the serious proceedings. (The *Merchant* is a comedy, but Shakespeare does this even in tragedies; the addition of 'for God's sake' is blatantly inappropriate, since Jesus forgave those who put him to death. The joke may also recall that, after betraying Jesus in return for money, Judas 'went and hanged himself' (Luke 27:5).) Ignoring Gratiano's foolery, Antonio speaks to the Duke with a composed courtesy remarkable in one who has just escaped the knife.

Antonio respects court procedure, asking the Duke to let Shylock off the state's half of Shylock's goods on condition that the other half, due to him, is accepted by him only as a non-profit-making trustee for Lorenzo and Jessica. He makes two further immediate conditions: that Shylock become a Christian; and that he make a will leaving everything to his daughter and her husband. The Duke imposes these conditions on penalty of life, and Shylock (after a silence?) accepts them.

Antonio's complex offer shows clemency. He refuses to make money out of Shylock's crime, and insists that the father's money goes to the daughter of his house. However, she has joyfully escaped from the house of bondage and is said to have prodigally wasted Shylock's 'Christian ducats' and family jewels. Her Christian husband will after Shylock's death be legal owner of the wealth that remains. The conditions are generous; but they sharply fit the crime.

Portia says little but skilfully directs all the proceedings. She asks for Shylock's reply. It is brief: 'I am content.' Even more surprising, he follows with: 'I pray you give me leave ...' – a change of tone. He is quiet and monosyllabic as he begs to leave. The Duke allows it, and Gratiano has a final jest.

What are we to make of Shylock's surrender and change of tone? The Christian terms are merciful – if you are a Christian, as Shakespeare and his audience were. A Jew would notice that Shylock is unwilling to die for his religion. Has all his talk been tribal ? Is money, religion or his daughter, the *prop* of his house? On the other side, Shakespeare complicates the issue by having Antonio call Lorenzo 'the gentleman / That lately *stole* his daughter'; we remember Jessica throwing down the casket. Antonio thinks of her future, and the Duke is dignified and unvindictive. The language and the verse of the Christians (apart from the yelps of Gratiano) are measured, courteous and civil. But they get back (eventually) all the money Shylock has made out of them. The financial aspect may also be hinted at in the word 'use' (= trust, in contrast to Shylock's usury). The sentence has two sides, like much in Shakespeare.

Forced conversion offends against modern liberal principle. But conversion was, according to Christian belief of the day, a prerequisite of salvation: it is therefore (**paradoxically**) charity. Antonio, who spat at Shylock, has been humbled, and he now returns good for Shylock's evil.

How should Shylock leave? Content to have got off lightly? A broken man? Or a humbled and wiser man? Will he live long?

TEXT 3      LORENZO AND JESSICA: A DUET

*Enter* LORENZO *and* JESSICA

LORENZO: The moon shines bright. In such a night as this,

When the sweet wind did gently kiss the trees,

And they did make no noise, in such a night

Troilus methinks mounted the Troyan walls

And sighed his soul toward the Grecian tents,

Where Cressid lay that night.

JESSICA:           In such a night

Did Thisbe fearfully o'ertrip the dew,

And saw the lion's shadow ere himself,
And ran dismayed away.

LORENZO:                    In such a night
Stood Dido with a willow in her hand
Upon the wild sea banks, and waft her love
To come again to Carthage.

JESSICA:                    In such a night
Medea gathered the enchanted herbs
That did renew old Aeson.

LORENZO:                    In such a night
Did Jessica steal from the wealthy Jew
And with an unthrift love did run from Venice
As far as Belmont.

JESSICA:              In such a night
Did young Lorenzo swear he loved her well,
Stealing her soul with many vows of faith,
And ne'er a true one.

LORENZO:              In such a night
Did pretty Jessica (like a little shrew)
Slander her love, and he forgave it her.

JESSICA: I would outnight you, did nobody come:
But hark, I hear the footing of a man.

*Enter* [STEPHANO,] *a messenger*

LORENZO: Who comes so fast in silence of the night?

STEPHANO: A friend.

LORENZO: A friend? What friend? Your name, I pray you, friend?

STEPHANO: Stephano is my name, and I bring word
My mistress will before the break of day
Be here at Belmont. She doth stray about
By holy crosses where she kneels and prays
For happy wedlock hours.

LORENZO:                    Who comes with her?

STEPHANO: None but a holy hermit and her maid.
I pray you, is my master yet returned?

LORENZO: He is not, nor we have not heard from him.
But go we in, I pray thee, Jessica,
And ceremoniously let us prepare
Some welcome for the mistress of the house.

*Enter* [LANCELOT,] *the Clown*

LANCELOT: Sola, sola! Wo ha, ho! Sola, sola!

LORENZO: Who calls?

LANCELOT: Sola! Did you see Master Lorenzo? Master Lorenzo, sola, sola!

LORENZO: Leave holloaing, man! Here!

LANCELOT: Sola! Where, where?

LORENZO: Here!

LANCELOT: Tell him there's a post come from my master, with his horn full of good news: my master will be here ere morning, sweet soul.

LORENZO: Let's in and there expect their coming.
And yet no matter: why should we go in?
My friend Stephano, signify I pray you,
Within the house, your mistress is at hand,
And bring your music forth into the air.

*[Exit Stephano]*

How sweet the moonlight sleeps upon this bank!
Here will we sit, and let the sounds of music
Creep in our ears; soft stillness and the night
Become the touches of sweet harmony.
Sit, Jessica. Look how the floor of heaven
Is thick inlaid with patens of bright gold.
There's not the smallest orb which thou behold'st
But in his motion like an angel sings,
Still choiring to the young-eyed cherubins.
Such harmony is in immortal souls,
But whilst this muddy vesture of decay
Doth grossly close it in, we cannot hear it. (V.1.1–63)

The lovers' conversation is in the musical form of a variation on a theme. The theme is 'The moon shines bright. In such a night as this...' (a line which itself has internal rhyme). Line 3 ends, 'in such a night' and the newly weds speak alternate speeches beginning 'In such a night' in lines 6, 9, 12, 14 and 16. They echo one another like cooing pigeons, or lovers in an opera. Each gives an instance of a silent night-scene from a famous classical love story. Moonlit nights and famous love stories create a romantic atmosphere, and the function of the scene is to change the key and the mood away from the drama of the trial towards the light-hearted 'trial' of Bassanio by Portia and Gratiano by Nerissa, ending in loving reconciliation.

The verse is blank (i.e., unrhymed), yet has 'in such a night' seven times, and rhymes 'dew' unromantically with 'Jew' and 'shrew'. The lines move smoothly and regularly, and employ patterns usually found only in nondramatic verse. A string of paired sounds repeats the pattern of the duet: 'no noise', 'Troilus ... Troyan', 'sighed his soul', 'Dido ... willow', 'wild ... waft', 'come ... Carthage', 'Jessica ... Jew', 'Lorenzo ... loved'. Each speech contains a lover's name or two, all taken from Ovid. The first three, also found in Chaucer, are unhappy stories of parted lovers: Cressid had to leave Troilus; Pyramus killed himself after mistakenly thinking Thisbe dead; Dido was deserted by Aeneas. Medea, an enchantress whose magic helped Jason to regain the Golden Fleece from her own father (see III.2.239), here renews her lover's aged father with a very powerful magic brew. This does not seem to go with the first three pairs, except that Medea robbed her father, like Jessica; she later deserted Jason. Aeson was old, and so is Shylock in the next instance, where a young witch 'gathers' something. She 'steals' (creeps away), but also steals gold which makes their 'unthrift' love a more thriving business. Jessica's response to her husband's teasing is that if she stole from her father, Lorenzo stole her soul from her with vows which were all untrue. Lorenzo forgives her; she says she could 'outnight' him but that someone is coming.

The names are famous, melodious and decorative, and that is probably their main function. They change the mood and prepare us for the introduction of music. An educated hearer or reader might, however, have reflected that, as well as love and silence, each instance has an element of unhappiness or infidelity. After Medea, Lorenzo switches teasingly to Jessica, and Jessica teases him back. With 'little shrew', romance gives way to good humour. There are serious touches: Medea helped Jason win the Golden Fleece, and Portia too is a kind of enchantress who helps her Jason strike gold, though with white rather than black magic. The financial theme is recalled again with 'wealthy' and 'unthrift'. Finally, Lorenzo steals Jessica's soul, with lovers' vows (proverbially false) but also persuades her Jewish soul to become a Christian soul; marital vows must be true. These themes give way on to the main business of the scene: wives showing their husbands Christian forgiveness for breaking their word.

Stephano's message does not break the mood, maintaining a 'romance' fiction of the holy bride and her pious maid. The shouts and jokes of the clown Lancelot broaden the humour without ruining the atmosphere. The musicians are heralded by a famous set-piece. Like 'The quality of mercy is not strained', 'How sweet the moonlight sleeps on yonder bank' is entirely serious (though it also has the tenderness of the playful and mischievous love duet which precedes it). The Christian Lorenzo instructs his newly Christian bride in the Christian-Platonic doctrine of the music of the spheres. Moonlight, softness and stillness are heralds not to earthly love and kisses but to an immortal celestial harmony beyond the reach of human ears. Eyes, however, can see the stars like 'patens of bright gold'. 'Patens' is a distinctly Christian reference to the small dishes used in the Communion service, which, seen from below, look like the golden bosses in an elaborate Elizabethan ceiling. The marriage of the Jew's daughter to a Christian is a **comedic** happy ending, pointing heavenwards. Also, in this wealthy play, they are going to inherit Shylock's earthly gold. There is something magical and arbitrary about the way Lorenzo is made such a wise young man in Belmont, but Belmont has had that effect on Bassanio too. At Belmont, the land of metamorphosis, the heartless Gratiano is lucky, and even Antonio has some luck at last.

# PART FIVE

# Background

## Shakespeare's life

There are no personal records of Shakespeare's life. Official documents and occasional references to him by contemporary dramatists enable us to draw the main outline of his public life, but his private life remains hidden. Although not at all unusual for a writer of his time, this lack of first-hand evidence has tempted many to read his plays as personal records and to look in them for clues to his character and convictions. The results are unconvincing, partly because Renaissance art was not subjective or designed primarily to express its creator's personality, and partly because the drama of any period is very difficult to read biographically. Except when plays are written by committed dramatists to promote social or political causes (as by Shaw or Brecht), it is all but impossible to decide who amongst the variety of fictional characters in a drama represents the dramatist, or which, if any, of the various and often conflicting points of view expressed is authorial.

What we do know can be quickly summarised. Shakespeare was born into a well-to-do family in the market town of Stratford-upon-Avon in Warwickshire, where he was baptised, in Holy Trinity Church, on 26 April 1564. His father, John Shakespeare, was a prosperous glover and leather merchant who became a person of some importance in the town: in 1565 he was elected an alderman of the town, and in 1568 he became high bailiff (or mayor) of Stratford, though his fortunes soon declined. In 1557 he had married Mary Arden. There is evidence that the family had Catholic sympathies. Their third child (of eight) and eldest son, William, learned to read and write at the primary (or 'petty') school in Stratford and then, it seems probable, attended the local grammar school, where he would have studied Latin, history, logic and rhetoric. In November 1582 William, then aged eighteen, married Anne Hathaway, who was twenty-six years old. They had a daughter, Susanna, in May 1583, and twins, Hamnet and Judith, in 1585.

Shakespeare next appears in the historical record in 1592 when he was mentioned as a London actor and playwright in a pamphlet by the dramatist Robert Greene. These 'lost years' 1585–92 have been the subject of speculation. The most likely theory is that he was a schoolmaster in Lancashire. But we do not know when Shakespeare left Stratford, nor why. In his pamphlet, *Greene's Groatsworth of Wit*, Greene expresses to his fellow dramatists his outrage that the 'upstart crow' Shakespeare has the impudence to believe he 'is as well able to bombast out a blank verse as the best of you'. To have aroused this hostility Shakespeare must, by 1592, have been long enough in London to have made a name for himself as a playwright.

During the next twenty years, Shakespeare continued to live in London, regularly visiting his wife and family in Stratford. He continued to act, but his chief fame was as a dramatist. From 1594 he wrote exclusively for the Lord Chamberlain's Men, which rapidly became the leading dramatic company and from 1603 enjoyed the patronage of James I as the King's Men. His plays were extremely popular and he became a shareholder in his theatre company. He was able to buy lands around Stratford and a large house in the town, to which he retired about 1611. He died there on 23 April 1616 and was buried in Holy Trinity Church on 25 April.

## HIS DRAMATIC CAREER

Between the late 1580s and 1613 Shakespeare wrote thirty-seven plays, and contributed to some by other dramatists. This was by no means an exceptional number for a professional playwright of the times. The exact date of the composition of individual plays is a matter of debate – for only a few plays is the date of their first performance known – but the broad outlines of Shakespeare's dramatic career have been established. He began in the late 1580s and early 1590s by rewriting earlier plays and working with plotlines inspired by the Classics. He concentrated on comedies (such as *The Comedy of Errors*, 1590–4, which derived from the Latin playwright Plautus) and plays dealing with English history (such as the three parts of *Henry VI*, 1589–92), though he also tried his hand at bloodthirsty revenge tragedy (*Titus Andronicus*, 1592–3, indebted to both Ovid and Seneca). During the 1590s Shakespeare developed his expertise in these kinds of play to write such comic masterpieces such as *A Midsummer Night's Dream* (1594–5) and *As You Like It* (1599–1600) and history plays such as *Henry IV* (1596–8) and *Henry V* (1598–9).

As the new century begins a new note is detectable. Plays such as *Troilus and Cressida* (1601–2) and *Measure for Measure* (1603–4), poised between comedy and tragedy, evoke complex responses. Because of their generic uncertainty and ambivalent tone such works are sometimes referred to as 'problem plays', but it is tragedy which comes to dominate the extraordinary sequence of masterpieces: *Hamlet* (1600–1), *Othello* (1602–4), *King Lear* (1605–6), *Macbeth* (1605–6) and *Antony and Cleopatra* (1606).

In the last years of his dramatic career, Shakespeare wrote a group of plays of a quite different kind. These 'romances', as they are often called, are in many ways the most remarkable of all his plays. The group comprises *Pericles* (1608), *Cymbeline* (1609–11), *The Winter's Tale* (1610–11) and *The Tempest* (1610–11). These plays (particularly *Cymbeline*) take up many of the situations and themes of the earlier dramas but in fantastical and exotic dramatic designs which, set in distant lands, covering large tracts of time and involving music, mime, dance and tableaux, have something of the qualities of masques and pageants. The situations which in the tragedies had led to disaster are here resolved: the great theme is restoration and reconciliation. Where in the tragedies Ophelia, Desdemona and Cordelia died, the daughters of these plays – Marina, Imogen, Perdita, Miranda – survive and are reunited with their parents and lovers.

## THE TEXTS OF SHAKESPEARE'S PLAYS

Nineteen of Shakespeare's plays were printed during his lifetime in what are called 'quartos' (books, each containing one play, and made up of sheets of paper each folded twice to make four leaves). Shakespeare, however, did not supervise the publication of these plays. This was not unusual. When a playwright had sold a play to a dramatic company he sold his rights in it: copyright belonged to whoever had possession of an actual copy of the text, and so consequently authors had no control over what happened their work. Anyone who could get hold of the text of a play might publish it if they wished. Hence, what found its way into print might be the author's copy, but it might be an actor's copy or prompt copy, perhaps cut or altered for performance; sometimes, actors (or even members of the audience) might publish what they could remember of the text. Printers, working without the benefit of the author's oversight, introduced their own errors, through misreading the manuscript for example, and by 'correcting' what seemed to them not to make sense.

In 1623 John Heminges and Henry Condell, two actors in Shakespeare's company, collected together texts of thirty-six of Shakespeare's plays (*Pericles* was omitted) and published them in a large folio (a book in which each sheet of paper is folded once in half, to give two leaves). This, the First Folio, was followed by later editions in 1632, 1663 and 1685. Despite its appearance of authority, however, the texts in the First Folio still present many difficulties, for there are printing errors and confused passages in the plays, and its texts can differ significantly from those of the earlier quartos, when these exist.

Shakespeare's texts have, then, been through a number of intermediaries. We do not have his authority for any one of his plays, and hence we cannot be certain exactly what it was that he wrote. Bibliographers, textual critics and editors have spent a great deal of effort on trying to get behind the errors, uncertainties and contradictions in the available texts to recover the plays as Shakespeare originally wrote them. What we read is the result of these efforts. Modern texts are what editors have constructed from the available evidence: they do not correspond exactly to any sixteenth- or seventeenth-century editions, nor to the text of an early performance of a Shakespeare play. Furthermore, these composite texts differ from each other, for different editors read the early texts differently and in some places come to different conclusions. A Shakespeare text is the product of a lot of editorial work.

Often, of course, its judgements embody, if not the personal prejudices of the editor, then the cultural preferences of the time in which he or she was working. Growing awareness of this has led some recent scholars to become sceptical about the idea of a 'perfect' text. Stanley Wells and Gary Taylor, the editors of the Oxford edition of *The Complete Works* (1988), point out that almost certainly the texts of Shakespeare's plays were altered in performance, and from one performance to another, so that there may never have been a single version. They note, too, that Shakespeare probably revised and rewrote some plays. They do not claim to print a definitive text of any play, but prefer what seems to them the 'more theatrical' version; and when there is a great difference between available versions, as with *King Lear*, they print two texts.

Shakespeare arrived in London at the very time that the Elizabethan period was poised to become the 'golden age' of English literature. Although Elizabeth reigned as queen from 1558 to 1603, the term 'Elizabethan' can be used very loosely in a literary sense to refer to the period 1580 to 1625, when the great works of the age were produced. (Sometimes the later part of this period is distinguished as 'Jacobean', from 'Jacobus', the Latin form of the name of the king who succeeded Elizabeth, James I of England and VI of Scotland, who reigned from 1603 to 1625.) The poet Edmund Spenser heralded this new age with his pastoral poem *The Shepheardes Calender* (1579). In his essay *An Apologie for Poetrie* (written about 1580, although not published until 1595), Sir Philip Sidney championed the imaginative power of the 'speaking picture of poesy', famously declaring that 'Nature never set forth the earth in so rich a tapestry as divers poets have done ... Her world is brazen, the poets only deliver a golden'.

Spenser and Sidney were part of that rejuvenating movement in European culture which since the nineteenth century has been known by the term *Renaissance*. Meaning literally *rebirth* it denotes a revival and redirection of artistic and intellectual endeavour which began in Italy in the fourteenth century in the poetry of Petrarch. It spread gradually northwards across Europe, and is first detectable in England in the early sixteenth century in the writings of the scholar and statesman Sir Thomas More and in the poetry of Sir Thomas Wyatt and Henry Howard, Earl of Surrey. Its keynote was a curiosity in thought which challenged old assumptions and traditions.

That spirit was fuelled by the rediscovery of many Classical texts and the culture of Greece and Rome. This fostered a confidence in human reason and in human potential which, in every sphere, challenged old convictions. The discovery of America and its peoples (Columbus had sailed in 1492) demonstrated that the world was a larger and stranger place than had been thought. The cosmological speculation of Copernicus (later confirmed by Galileo) that the sun, not the earth was the centre of our planetary system challenged the ancient belief that the earth and human beings were at the centre of the cosmos. The pragmatic political philosophy of Machiavelli seemed to cut politics free from its traditional link with morality by permitting to statesmen any means which secured the desired end. And the religious movements we know collectively as the Reformation broke with the Church of Rome and set the individual conscience, not ecclesiastical authority, at the centre of the religious life. Nothing, it seemed, was beyond questioning, nothing impossible.

Shakespeare's drama is innovative and challenging in the way of the Renaissance. It questions the beliefs, assumptions and politics upon which Elizabethan society was founded. And although the plays always conclude in a restoration of order and stability, many recent critics argue that their imaginative energy goes into questioning, rather than reinforcing, traditional values. They point out that the famous speech on hierarchical order in *Troilus and Cressida* (I.3.86–124) or Katerina's speech on wifely submission to patriarchal authority in *The Taming of the Shrew* (V.2.146–60) appear to be rendered **ironic** by the action of the plays in which they occur. Convention, audience expectation and censorship all required the *status quo* to be endorsed by the plots' conclusions, but the dramas find ways to allow alternative sentiments to be expressed. Frequently, figures of authority are undercut by some **comic or parodic** figure: against the Duke in *Measure for Measure* is set Lucio; against Prospero in *The Tempest*, Caliban; against Henry IV, Falstaff. Despairing, critical, dissident, disillusioned, unbalanced, rebellious, mocking voices can be heard in the plays, rejecting, resenting, defying the established order. They often belong to marginal, socially unacceptable figures, 'licensed', as it were, by their situations to say what would be unacceptable from socially privileged or responsible citizens. Are such characters given these views to discredit them, or were they the only ones through whom a voice could be given to radical and dissident ideas?

Renaissance culture was often nationalistic. With the break-up of the internationalism of the Middle Ages the evolving nation states which still mark the map of Europe began for the first time to acquire distinctive cultural identities. There was intense rivalry among them as they sought to achieve in their own vernacular languages a culture which could equal that of Greece and Rome. Spenser's great allegorical epic poem *The Faerie Queene*, which began to appear from 1590, celebrated Elizabeth and was intended to outdo the poetic achievements of France and Italy and to stand beside works of Virgil and Homer. Shakespeare is also concerned with national identity. His history plays tell an epic story which examines how modern England came into being through the conflicts of the fifteenth-century Wars of the Roses which brought the Tudors to the throne. He is fascinated, too, by the related subject of politics and the exercise of power. With the collapse of medieval feudalism and the authority of local barons, the royal court in the Renaissance came to assume a new status as the centre of power and patronage. It was here that the destiny of a country was shaped. Courts, and how to succeed in them, consequently fascinated the Renaissance; and they fascinated Shakespeare and his audience.

That is why we are usually at court in his plays, and in the company of courtiers. But the dramatic gaze is not merely admiring; through a variety of devices, a critical perspective is brought to bear. The court may be paralleled by a very different world, revealing comical similarities (for example, Henry's court and the Boar's Head tavern, ruled over by Falstaff in *Henry IV*). Its hypocrisy may be bitterly denounced (for example, in the diatribes of the mad Lear) and its self-seeking ambition represented disturbingly in the figure of a Machiavellian villain (such as Edmund in *Lear*) or a malcontent (such as Iago in *Othello*). Shakespeare is fond of displacing the court to another context, the better to examine its assumptions and pretensions and to offer alternatives to the courtly life (for example, in the pastoral setting of the forest of Arden in *As You Like It* or Prospero's island in *The Tempest*). Courtiers are frequently figures of fun whose unmanly sophistication ('neat and trimly dressed, / Fresh as a bridegroom ... perfumed like a milliner', says Hotspur of such a man in *Henry IV*, I.3.33–6) is contrasted with plain-speaking integrity: Oswald is set against Kent in *King Lear*.

(When thinking of these matters, we should remember that stage plays were subject to censorship, and any criticism had therefore to be muted or oblique: direct criticism of the monarch or the contemporary English court would not be tolerated. This has something to do with why the plays are set either in the past, or abroad.)

The nationalism of the English Renaissance was reinforced by Protestantism. Henry VIII had broken with Rome in the 1530s and Queen Elizabeth established a Protestant state church. Because the Pope had excommunicated Elizabeth as a heretic and relieved the English of their allegiance to the Crown, there was government suspicion of Roman Catholics as potential traitors. There was persecution of Catholics in Warwickshire. The Spanish Armada of 1588 was a crusade to restore England to Roman Catholic allegiance; Catholicism was hence easily associated with disloyalty and treachery. Shakespeare's plays, although generally Christian and even at times sacramental, are remarkably free from sectarian sentiment, although Puritans, extreme Protestants, are portrayed as ridiculous: for example, Malvolio in *Twelfth Night*.

The central figures of the plays are frequently individuals beset by temptation, by the lure of evil – Angelo in *Measure for Measure*, Othello, Lear, Macbeth. We follow their inner struggles. Shakespeare's heroes have the preoccupation with self and the introspective tendencies encouraged by Protestantism: his tragic heroes are haunted by their consciences, seeking their true selves, agonising over what course of action to take as they follow what can often be understood as a kind of spiritual progress towards heaven or hell.

## SHAKESPEARE'S THEATRE

The theatre for which the plays were written was one of the most remarkable innovations of the Renaissance. Although civic drama had flourished since the fourteenth century, and continued until Shakespeare's childhood, there had been no theatres in the medieval period. Performed on carts and in open spaces at Christian festivals, plays had been almost exclusively religious. Some professional actors wandered the country putting on entertainments in the yards of inns, on makeshift stages in market squares, or anywhere else suitable. They did not perform full-length plays, but mimes, juggling and comedy acts. Such actors were regarded by officialdom as little better than vagabonds.

Just before Shakespeare went to London all this began to change. A number of young men who had been to the universities of Oxford and Cambridge came to London in the 1580s and began to write plays which made use of what they had learned about the Classical drama of ancient Greece and Rome. Plays such as John Lyly's *Alexander and Campaspe* (1584), Christopher Marlowe's *Tamburlaine the Great* (about 1587) and Thomas Kyd's *The Spanish Tragedy* (1588–9) were unlike anything that had been written in English before. They were full-length plays on secular subjects, taking their plots from history and legend, adopting many of the devices of Classical drama, and offering a range of characterisation and situation hitherto unattempted in English drama. With the exception of Lyly's prose dramas, they were in the unrhymed iambic pentameters (blank verse) which the Earl of Surrey had introduced into English earlier in the sixteenth century. This was a freer and more expressive medium than the rhymed verse of medieval drama. It was the drama of these 'university wits' which Shakespeare challenged when he came to London. Greene was one of them, and we have heard how little he liked this Shakespeare setting himself up as a dramatist.

The most significant change of all, however, was that these dramatists wrote for the professional theatre. In 1576 James Burbage built the first permanent theatre in England, in Shoreditch, just beyond London's northern boundary. It was called simply 'The Theatre'. Others soon followed. Thus, when Shakespeare came to London, there was a flourishing drama, theatres and companies of actors waiting for him, such as there had never been before in England. His company performed at James Burbage's Theatre until 1596, and used the Swan and Curtain until they moved into their own new theatre, The Globe, in 1599. It was burned down in 1613 when a cannon was fired during a performance of Shakespeare's *Henry VIII*.

With the completion in 1996 of Sam Wanamaker's project to construct in London a replica of The Globe, and with productions now running there, a version of Shakespeare's theatre can be experienced at first-hand. It is very different to the usual modern experience of drama. The form of the Elizabethan theatre derived from the inn yards and animal-baiting rings in which actors had been accustomed to perform in the past. They were circular wooden buildings with a paved courtyard in the middle open to the sky. A rectangular stage jutted out into the middle of this yard. Much of the audience stood in the yard (or 'pit') to watch the play. They were thus on three sides of the stage, close up to it and on a level with it. These 'groundlings' paid only a penny to get in, but for wealthier spectators there were seats in three covered tiers or galleries between the inner and outer walls of the building, extending round most of the auditorium and overlooking the pit and the stage. Such a theatre could hold about 3,000 spectators. The yards were just over 24 metres in diameter and the rectangular stage approximately 12 metres by 9 metres and 1.67 metres high. Shakespeare aptly called such a theatre a 'wooden O' in the Prologue to *Henry V* (line 13).

The stage itself was partially covered by a roof or canopy which pro-jected from the wall at the rear of the stage and was supported by two posts

THE GLOBE THEATRE,

On the Bankside.

As it appeared in the reign of King James I.

## A CONJECTURAL RECONSTRUCTION OF THE INTERIOR OF THE GLOBE PLAYHOUSE

AA  Main entrance
B    The Yard
CC  Entrances to lowest galleries
D    Entrance to staircase and upper galleries
E    Corridor serving the different sections of the middle gallery
F    Middle gallery ('Twopenny Rooms')
G    'Gentlemen's Rooms or Lords Rooms'
H    The stage
J    The hanging being put up round the stage
K    The 'Hell' under the stage
L    The stage trap, leading down to the Hell
MM Stage doors

N    Curtained 'place behind the stage'
O    Gallery above the stage, used as required sometimes by musicians, sometimes by spectators, and often as part of the play
P    Back-stage area (the tiring-house)
Q    Tiring-house door
R    Dressing-rooms
S    Wardrobe and storage
T    The hut housing the machine for lowering enthroned gods, etc., to the stage
U    The 'Heavens'
W   Hoisting the playhouse flag

at the front. This protected the stage and performers from inclement weather, and to it were secured winches and other machinery for stage effects. On either side at the back of the stage was a door. These led into the dressing room (or 'tiring house') and it was by means of these doors that actors entered and left the stage. Between these doors was a small recess or alcove which was curtained off. Such a 'discovery place' served, for example, for Juliet's bedroom when in Act IV Scene 4 of *Romeo and Juliet* the Nurse went to the back of the stage and drew the curtain to find, or 'discover' in Elizabethan English, Juliet apparently dead on her bed. Above the discovery place was a balcony, used for the famous balcony scenes of *Romeo and Juliet* (II.2 and III.5), and for Jessica to throw the casket from in *The Merchant*. Actors (all parts in the Elizabethan theatre were taken by boys or men) had access to the area beneath the stage; from here, in the 'cellarage', would have come the voice of the ghost of Hamlet's father (*Hamlet*, II.1.150–82).

On these stages there was very little in the way of scenery or props – there was nowhere to store them (there were no wings in this theatre) nor any way to set them up (no tabs across the stage), and, anyway, productions had to be transportable for performance at court or at noble houses. The stage was bare, which is why characters often tell us where they are: there was nothing on the stage to indicate location. It is also why location is so rarely topographical, and much more often symbolic. It suggests a dramatic mood or situation, rather than a place: Lear's barren heath reflects his destitute state, as the storm his emotional turmoil.

None of the plays printed in Shakespeare's lifetime marks Act or scene divisions. These have been introduced by later editors, but they should not mislead us into supposing that there was any break in Elizabethan performances such as might happen today while the curtains are closed and the set is changed. The staging of Elizabethan plays was continuous, with the many short 'scenes' of which Shakespeare's plays are often constructed following one after another in quick succession. We have to think of a more fluid and much faster production than we are generally used to: in the prologues to *Romeo and Juliet* (line 12) and *Henry VIII* (line 13) Shakespeare speaks of only two hours as the playing time. It is because plays were staged continuously that exits and entrances are written in as part of the script: characters speak as they enter or leave the stage because otherwise there would be a silence while, in full view, they took up their positions. (This is also why dead bodies are carried off: they cannot get up and walk off.)

In 1608 Shakespeare's company, the King's Men, acquired the Blackfriars Theatre, a smaller, rectangular indoor theatre, holding about 700 people, with seats for all the members of the audience, facilities for elaborate stage effects and, because it was enclosed, artificial lighting. It has been suggested that the plays written for this 'private' theatre differed from those written for The Globe, since, as it cost more to go to a private theatre, the audience came from a higher social stratum and demanded the more elaborate and courtly entertainment which Shakespeare's romances provide. However, the King's Men continued to play in The Globe in the summer, using Blackfriars in the winter, and it is not certain that Shakespeare's last plays were written specifically for the Blackfriars Theatre, or first performed there.

## READING SHAKESPEARE

Shakespeare's plays were written for this stage, but there is also a sense in which they were written *by* this stage. The material and physical circumstances of their production in such theatres had a profound effect upon the nature of Elizabethan plays. Unless we bear this in mind, we are likely to find them very strange, for we will read with expectations shaped by our own familiarity with modern fiction and modern drama. This is, by and large, realistic; it seeks to persuade us that what we are reading or watching is really happening. This is quite foreign to Shakespeare. If we try to read him like this, we shall find ourselves irritated by the improbabilities of his plot, confused by his chronology, puzzled by locations, frustrated by unanswered questions and dissatisfied by the motivation of the action. The absurd ease with which disguised persons pass through Shakespeare's plays is a case in point: why does no-one recognise people they know so well? There is a great deal of psychological accuracy in Shakespeare's plays, but we are far from any attempt at realism.

The reason is that in Shakespeare's theatre it was impossible to pretend that the audience was not watching a contrived performance. In a modern theatre, the audience is encouraged to forget itself as it becomes absorbed by the action on stage. The worlds of the spectators and of the actors are sharply distinguished by the lighting: in the dark auditorium the audience is passive, silent, anonymous, receptive and attentive; on the lighted stage the actors are active, vocal, demonstrative and dramatic. (The distinction is still more marked in the cinema.) There is no communication between the two worlds: for the audience to speak would be to interrupt; for the actors to address the audience would be to break the illusion of the play. In the Elizabethan theatre, this distinction did not exist, and for two reasons: first, performances took place in the open air and in daylight which illuminated everyone; secondly, the spectators were all around the stage (wealthier spectators could be on it), and were dressed no differently to the actors, who wore contemporary dress. In such a theatre, spectators would be as aware of each other as of the actors; they could not lose their identity in a corporate group, nor could they ever forget that they were spectators at a performance. There was no chance that they could believe 'this is really happening'.

This, then, was communal theatre, not only in the sense that it was going on in the middle of a crowd but in the sense that the crowd joined in. Elizabethan audiences had little deference: they did not keep quiet, or arrive on time, or remain for the whole performance. They joined in, interrupted, even getting on the stage. And plays were preceded and followed by jigs and clowning. It was all much more like our experience of a pantomime, and at a pantomime we are fully aware, and are meant to be aware, that we are watching games being played with reality. The conventions of pantomime revel in their own artificiality: the fishnet tights are to signal that the handsome prince is a woman, the Dame's monstrous false breasts signal that 'she' is a man.

Something very similar is the case with Elizabethan theatre: it utilised its very theatricality. Instead of trying to persuade spectators that they are not in a theatre watching a performance, Elizabethan plays acknowledge the audience. It is addressed not only by prologues, epilogues and choruses, but in soliloquies. There is no realistic reason why characters should suddenly explain themselves to empty rooms, but, of course, it is not an empty room. The actor is surrounded by people. Soliloquies are not addressed to the world of the play: they are for the audience's benefit. And that audience's complicity is assumed: when a character like Prospero declares himself to be invisible, it is accepted that he is. Disguises are taken to be impenetrable, however improbable, and we are to accept impossibly contrived situations, such as barely hidden characters remaining undetected (indeed, on the Elizabethan stage there was nowhere they could hide).

These, then, are plays which are aware of themselves as dramas; in critical terminology, they are self-reflexive, commenting upon themselves as dramatic pieces and prompting the audience to think about the theatrical experience. They do this not only through their direct address to the audience but through their fondness for the play-within-a-play and their constant use of images from, and allusions to, the theatre. They are fascinated by role playing, by acting, appearance and reality. Things are rarely what they seem, either in comedy (for example, in *A Midsummer Night's Dream*) or tragedy (*Romeo and Juliet*). This offers one way to think about those disguises: they are thematic rather than realistic. Kent's disguise in *Lear* reveals his true, loyal self, while Edmund, who is not disguised, hides his true self. In *As You Like It*, Rosalind is more truly her female self when disguised as a man than when dressed as a woman.

The effect of all this is to confuse the distinction we would make between 'real life' and 'acting'. The case of Rosalind, for example, raises searching questions about gender roles, about how far it is 'natural' to be womanly or manly: how does the stage, on which a man can play a woman playing a man (and have a man fall in love with him/her), differ from life, in which we assume the roles we think appropriate to masculine and feminine behaviour? The same is true of political roles: when a Richard II or Lear is so aware of the regal part he is performing, of the trappings and rituals of kingship, their plays raise the uncomfortable possibility that the answer to the question, what constitutes a successful king, is simply: a good actor. Indeed, human life generally is repeatedly rendered through the imagery of the stage, from Macbeth's 'Life's but a walking shadow, a poor player / That struts and frets his hour upon the stage / And then is heard no more ...' (V.5.23–5) to Prospero's paralleling of human life to a performance which, like the globe (both world and theatre) will end (IV.1.146–58). When life is a fiction, like this play, or this play is a fiction like life, what is the difference? 'All the world's a stage ...' (*As You Like It*, II.7.139).

## SOURCES

Shakespeare made the story of his play by combining elements from several sources and analogues, changing and adding important details of his own:

### 1

A lost play called *The Jew* (*c*.1578), reported by Stephen Gosson to represent 'the greediness of worldly choosers, and bloody minds of usurers'.

### 2

The story of Giannetto in *Il Pecorone* (The Muttonhead), a collection of fifty tales modelled on the *Decameron* of Boccaccio, by a fourteenth-century contemporary of Geoffrey Chaucer, Ser Giovanni of Florence, printed in 1558 in Italian. This has two Venetian friends, a loan, a Lady of Belmonte, a flesh-bond with a Jew, the Lady disguised as lawyer, a trial which turns upon taking exactly one pound of flesh without a drop of blood, a bridal ring trick, and a final marriage.

### 3

Christopher Marlowe's *The Jew of Malta* (*c*.1589): the protagonist Barabas is a forcefully ingenious trickster-villain, who blows up a convent of nuns in which his daughter Abigail (who loves a Christian) has taken refuge. The father-daughter relationship is a parallel with that of Shylock and Jessica. The wicked Barabas is more enjoyable than his Christian opponents.

### 4

The thirty-second History of the medieval *Gesta Romanorum* has a choice of caskets leading to marriage, with many similarities to Shakespeare's; but the chooser is a woman.

### 5

The fourteenth story of Masuccio's *Il Novellino* (1476): a miser's daughter elopes, taking his money with her (like Jessica; but neither is Jewish).

6

Anthony Munday's prose tale *Zelauto* (1580) has two lovers, a money-lender, a flesh-bond, two ladies dressed up as lawyers, no drop of blood to be shed, a double wedding.

7

A ballad of *Gernutus*, a Jew foiled of his bond, of roughly the same time as *The Merchant*.

8

Alexandre Silvain's *The Orator*, translated from the French, probably by Munday (see 6 above), 1596. His Declamation 95, 'Of a Jew, who would for his debt have a pound of flesh of a Christian' has arguments similar to those used in the Trial Scene.

Of these, 2 and 3 are most important, followed by 4, 6 and 8. In *Il Pecorone*, Giannetto is the adopted son (not the younger friend) of a wealthy Venetian, Ansaldo. The Lady of Belmonte wants Giannetto to sleep with her but drugs his drink: his ship is forfeit. She tries him again and he fails again. At the third attempt, a servant-girl warns Giannetto about the drink; this time he succeeds in sleeping with the Lady. Ansaldo had financed the first two expeditions but borrows money from a Jew for the third. The forfeit is a pound of flesh, but the disguised Lady/lawyer foils the wicked Jew and plays the ring-trick on Giannetto. Ansaldo marries the servant-girl. The similarities are striking, but so are Shakespeare's changes (his Lady is ideally virtuous), and his additions: the caskets, the elopement of Jessica, the doubling of the ring-trick, and much else. The Italian source is comic, thin and crude in comparison.

Shakespeare liked to find his ingredients in existing stories, and to combine, change and transform, inventing only when he had to. He enriched what he took with new motifs, ideas and feelings, producing complexity of theme. By this stage in his career, his resources of mind, verse and language give his plays an orchestral quality, with theme and motif echoed everywhere.

*Il Pecorone* is a prose tale, but Marlowe's *Jew of Malta* is a play and a masterpiece. The original and forceful Marlowe dominated the London stage for ten years; he was killed in 1594. Shakespeare's *Richard II*, composed at much the same time as his *Merchant*, owes much to Marlowe's

*Edward II.* Shakespeare admired and learned from Marlowe, but he had a very different kind of mind and did not copy. Marlowe's play concerns a Jew and his daughter who loves a Christian; and pits Jew against Christian. But *The Jew of Malta* mixes tragic farce and heartless comedy with cynical satire on the greed of Christian, Turk and Jew. Barabas is a comic villain superior in intelligence to Christian and Turk. Marlowe's play thus lacks romance, poetry and any interest in loving and giving. Yet its Barabas is wonderfully compelling.

# HISTORICAL BACKGROUND

## JEWS AND CHRISTIANS

The Jews are God's chosen people, according to the book of Genesis, the first book in the Hebrew Scriptures, the Old Testament of the Christian Bible. Christians believe that the Saviour or Messiah looked forward to by the Jewish prophets in the Old Testament is Jesus, the Christ, and that he is the Son of God. The New Testament of the Bible reports that Jesus was rejected and crucified at the insistence of the Jewish mob: 'Then answered all the people, and said, His blood be on us, and on our children' (Matthew 27:25). The destruction of Jerusalem by the Romans in AD70 was interpreted by medieval Christians as retribution for the killing of the Messiah. In the Middle Ages, Jews left Israel in the Diaspora (scattering) and spread over the Old World, living in cities in separate communities distinguished by religion, by ritual, hygiene and diet, and by dress. Judaism kept Jews ethnically distinct, for a Jew is the child of a Jewish mother: marrying a non-Jew is forbidden, and Jews do not seek converts. One can become a Jew only by birth or marrying a Jew and converting, whereas Christianity is international and non-racial. As aliens and non-citizens, medieval Jews could not own land, and often worked as jewellers and moneylenders (an unpopular profession); a few became rich. Jews lent money to the King; they thus provided a useful but disreputable service. Christians believed (a belief now held in a more liberal sense) that salvation is only by baptism, and that Jews cannot be saved except by Christian conversion and baptism. Yet the Jews, the Chosen People, are not like other non-Christians, and it is part of Christian tradition that the world will not end until the conversion of the Jews.

## USURY

In the Old Testament, the exacting of interest on a loan was forbidden to Jews who were lending to Jews. In the Middle Ages it was forbidden to Christian clerics, and then to laymen, although in 1215 a Council of the Church allowed Jews to take interest. In medieval theory, money was a medium of exchange. Aristotle had taught that money could not breed money: it was 'barren' (Antonio's argument in Act I Scene 3). After the rise of capitalism, the sixteenth-century reformers relaxed this teaching; Calvin permitted the taking of interest, and in England in 1571 moderate interest was no longer prohibited by civil law. In the 1650s Oliver Cromwell permitted Jews to return to England. In Catholic countries toleration of usury came late; not in France until 1789. Islam still forbids usury. Shylock is a usurer, whereas Antonio is a merchant venturer, a new and glamorous occupation in Elizabethan England. We know that Shakespeare, a financial partner in his own theatre company, also invested in the Company which developed Virginia.

The practice of giving credit and charging interest, the basis of modern banking, developed in the trading cities of Europe after AD1100, especially in the cities of Lombardy in northern Italy (hence Lombard St, a bankers' street in the City of London). Jewish lenders were dependent on royal favour, and kings sometimes repudiated their debts to Jews.

## ANTI-SEMITISM

In 1290 King Edward I banished Jews from England. Thereafter they did not live openly in England; a few stayed on, converting or apparently conforming to Christianity. English people knew Jews only from legend. In the popular medieval Mystery Plays, which lasted until Shakespeare's youth, Jews featured as a cursed race. It was rumoured that they killed children and drank their blood. In the legend of little St Hugh of Lincoln (Chaucer's Prioress's Tale), Jews murder a Christian child.

An association with anti-Semitic legends of ritual sacrifice is half-suggested in the trial scene by Shylock's knife. The Jewish Paschal feast involves the sacrifice of a lamb, whereas in Christian belief Christ at his last Paschal supper instituted the Eucharist as an unbloody sacrifice. Christians see Christ as the final sacrificial scapegoat.

Despite what popular Christianity may have thought, Judaism has always been against human sacrifice. God made it clear to the patriarch Abraham that he demanded obedience not sacrifice: once Abraham had shown willingness to sacrifice Isaac, God provided a ram to sacrifice instead (Genesis 24–28). Animal sacrifice was later regarded by Jewish spiritual writers as an external if necessary observance. But the Gospels begin with Herod's massacre of the innocents (Jews killing children), and end with the Crucifixion. St Paul, a Jew, encouraged Christians to regard Judaism as bound by the Old Law of justice, and themselves, whether Jewish or Gentile, as bound by the New Law of love. This bears on the contest of justice and mercy, retaliation and forgiveness, a theme of the play (see Themes). Despite these entrenched prejudices, stage Jews could also become caricature figures of fun and fantastic mischief as well as of hostility, as in Marlowe's Barabas.

Anti-Semitism has often been regarded as sinful, since Christianity developed out of Judaism. Semites are the sons of Shem, one of Noah's three sons, from whom humanity descends. In biblical tradition, the inhabitants of the region of Palestine, Arab as well as Jew, descend from Shem. Despite its etymology, 'anti-Semitism' means prejudice against Jews rather than against Levantines in general. And despite official Christian teaching, European history has been disfigured by discrimination against Jews. Jews were tolerated in England in the later seventeenth century, and allowed to work in the City of London. This gradually affected the reception of *The Merchant of Venice*. A new phase was opened in 1945, when the full horrors of the Nazi genocide of Jews became undeniable public knowledge (see Critical History).

## VENICE

Venice was a city which fascinated the Elizabethans, who set many plays in Italy; Venice is the setting for *Othello*, as for Ben Jonson's play *Volpone* (1606). Shakespeare need not have visited Venice, for she had long been known to English travellers as the port to the East; Venice transported Crusaders, and transported and insured pilgrims to Jerusalem. Unlike England, Venice was not a nation ruled by a king but an ancient civic republic, commercially hospitable to foreigners from east, west and north, Greek, Jew or Protestant. Physically remarkable, built on a set of islands, a unique, dignified, artistic, luxurious and splendid city, she was Catholic but politically independent. Like England, she was insular and dependent on sea-borne trade. Venice's credit was good by reason of her reputation for strictly enforcing her laws, even against her citizens. The word of a merchant of Venice was his bond. Venice was at one end of the chain of mercantile cities in Europe, London at the other; both were centres of marine insurance and venture capital. Jews were tolerated in Venice, and lived in the original (walled) Ghetto, not mentioned by Shakespeare. The exoticism of Venice is seen at Belmont, a palatial estate of vague location. It can be reached by sailing, and also by the 'traject', the 'common ferry which trades to Venice'; the ferry point is twenty miles from Belmont, hence presumably on the Venetian mainland of Italy rather than on an island. The less exotic business of Venice is seen at its centre, on the Rialto. Shakespeare used all these ideas about Venice in his play, though he set it, consciously or not, in the days of its greatest prosperity around 1500.

# PART SIX

# CRITICAL HISTORY

Apart from theoretical and political approaches, three scholarly approaches have altered our understanding of Shakespeare recently: bibliography; stage history; and the history of critical reception.

## BIBLIOGRAPHY

Bibliography, the physical study of the printing of the texts in order to get closer to what Shakespeare wrote, does not much affect *The Merchant*, for its existing texts hardly differ: Shylock is sometimes 'Jew' in speech-prefixes, and sometimes 'Shylock'. And if the quarto edition's title page advertises 'the extreame crueltie of *Shylocke* the Iewe', these are the words of a bookseller, not of the author. Guesses at Shakespeare's attitudes have to be based on his writings. All we have is a play-text, close to that of early performances.

## STAGE HISTORY

If we turn to stage history, the early record is scanty. It was performed 'divers times' before 1600, probably in 1596–7; and then at court before James I in 1605. The king asked for it again two days later, on Shrove Tuesday, the festive day before Lent. We hear of no further performance until 1741, although in 1701 it was used as the basis of *The Jew of Venice* by Granville, much cut and rewritten, with Shylock as comic villain, but as the focal figure. In 1741 a more restored version, with Shylock as a fierce villain, began the play's popularity. In 1814 Kean made Shylock more humane. Various versions then held the stage, cut and adapted to suit the needs of a changing theatre, including the unchanging need for money. The actor Henry Irving privately described Shylock as 'a bloody-minded monster'. But that is not how he chose to play Shylock in his lavish revival of the play with Ellen Terry as Portia in 1879. His own Shylock returned home in Act II to knock on the door of an empty house; and Act V was dropped. Shylock was the 'type of a persecuted race; almost the only gentleman in the play, and most ill-used.' Portia was womanly and full of warmth. Irving's version ran for 250 nights.

A less sentimental Victorian production had Shylock as a **comic** villain in a red wig, a usurer whose Jewishness is incidental. An Antonio of 1932 was a decadent and his friends bourgeois idlers. In 1933 Hitler came to power, since when Shylock has not often been the villain of the piece. In 1970 Jonathan Miller produced a gentlemanly assimilated Jew (Laurence Olivier), cutting 'I hate him for he is a Christian'. Jewish directors and actors usually make his Jewishness central; yet he can be a Jew of different kinds: an unassimilated oriental Jew; a central European Jew with a Yiddish accent; or a Jew who is content to change his religion if he can keep some money. The first of these can be found in the text. But the text has nothing to say about some things. Settings can be Elizabethan, Victorian, or modern Italian; Antonio can be made openly homosexual; swastikas can be painted on the walls. What works in the theatre depends on time, place and fashion. In Nazi Germany the play was used as anti-Jewish propaganda. That is not the way it is done in modern Germany or New York or Israel, or in Australia or Japan, or modern England.

Stage history suggests that the millions of people who have seen the play since James I have rarely heard the words in the texts we read. The stage does not have a literary critic's respect for the text. It is only a script for acting; if the text presents a problem, it can be changed or cut. Stage history shows that over four centuries any cultural phenomenon will change a good deal. If by some miracle the performance James I saw were put on at the 'authentic' Globe (opened in 1996), the audience would not be authentic Jacobeans. The play James I saw would seem different to them, and it would thereby become a rather different play.

It is not only theatre-goers who have changed. Those who read the play without seeing it have also changed. But they read the text rather than have the theatre interpret it for them. A careful reading of the text can prevent the more perverse kinds of misinterpretation. Yet there is no single right reading of a play, for it dramatises several voices, none of them the author's. A play is like a tennis match without an umpire; there is no superior fixed viewpoint.

## CRITICAL RECEPTION

There is little criticism of single plays before the 1707 edition of Shakespeare by Nicholas Rowe, a man of the theatre, who wrote of:

> that incomparable character of Shylock the Jew, in *The Merchant of Venice*, but though we have seen that play received and acted as a comedy, and the part of the Jew performed by an excellent comedian, yet I cannot but think it was designed tragically by the author. There appears in it such a deadly spirit of revenge, such a savage fierceness and fellness, and such a bloody designation of cruelty and mischief, as cannot agree either with the style or characters of comedy.

Rowe shows the neoclassical liking of his day for purity of genre. He forgets however that tragedy requires that we should admire the protagonist rather than feel sorry for him. Perhaps Rowe's comments helped to push the 1741 production in a tragic direction. Rowe continued:

> The play itself, take it all together, seems to me to be one of the most finished of any of Shakespear's. The tale, indeed, in that part relating to the caskets, and the extravagant and unusual kind of bond given by Antonio, is a little too much removed from the rules of probability: but taking the fact for granted, we must allow it to be very beautifully written. There is something in the friendship of Antonio to Bassanio very great, generous, and tender.

William Hazlitt in his *Characters of Shakespeare's Plays* (1818) wrote:

> In proportion as Shylock has ceased to be a popular bugbear, 'baited with the rabble's curse,' he becomes a half-favourite with the philosophical part of the audience, who are disposed to think that Jewish revenge is at least as good as Christian injuries. Shylock is *a good hater*, 'a man no less sinned against than sinning'.

Hazlitt added, however, that 'The stage is not in general the best place to study our author's characters in. It is too often filled with traditional commonplace conceptions of the part, handed down from sire to son.' Hazlitt assumes that Shylock is the central figure, reflecting the fact that his passionate speeches tend to dominate the theatre. In the theatre, and in literature since the eighteenth-century's cult of Feeling, intensity of feeling can have more impact than the ethics or conduct of the speaker.

After 1800 the chief change in critical reception, as in theatrical reception, is that Shylock has become not only the focus but the focus of sympathy. Since he was originally, at least to some extent, a comic butt, this unbalances the **comedic** design of the play. Although nineteenth-century critics see that he openly expresses hatred, greed and vengefulness, they are affected by the changing climate of opinion. Religious toleration and respect for individual rights were now widespread ideals; Hazlitt's 'philosophical part' of society felt sorry for the oppressed and the excluded. In the twentieth century, notions of European superiority have been shaken, not least by Hitler's policy of genocide against Jews and others. This makes some historical facts a cause for scandal, notably that for centuries an intense dislike of Jews was widespread in England; and others harder to accept, notably the historic Christian doctrines that only Jews who converted could be saved, and that the world could not end until all Jews had been converted.

The critic and the theatre director embarrassed by the historical anti-Semitism of *The Merchant* react in several ways. They can minimise the problem by making the play an unrealistic fairytale or by making Shylock more of a usurer than a Jew. More commonly, they maximise the humanity of Shylock and show anti-Semitism as evil. If as a result the Christians are made not only imperfect but wicked, a worse distortion is created. Although Antonio spits at Shylock, he is ultimately merciful. Some of his young friends prefer golden girls, and others mock Shylock's misfortune. Yet Bassanio remains the hero of the romance (in theatrical terms, the 'young male lead'), and Portia is both the heroine of the romantic comedy and the hero of the trial. One conclusion might be that *The Merchant* is so balanced and interrelated that to maximise or minimise any element, in order to make the play morally consistent or one-sided or unambiguous or politically correct for the year 2000, is to reduce its many-sidedness and to iron out its variety of perspectives.

How does this sketch of the course of critical reception help us? It makes us realise that texts change with time and audience. To sum up on Shylock: Shakespeare makes Shylock's Jewishness real to us. Perhaps Shakespeare was dissatisfied with the caricature stage Jew of the flesh-bond story and of Marlowe's *Jew of Malta*. His source-story and his rival's play were intrinsically anti-Semitic, and Shakespeare, however humane, was not above all the prejudices of his time and place. If the story of *The Merchant* is intrinsically anti-Semitic, the play is also *about* anti-Semitism. If Christian mistrust of Jews was racial, religious and commercial, their mistreatment of Jews leads to revenge. Although Shylock's actions are hateful, we can understand some of his feelings. But if Shakespeare considerably humanised his Jew, he still had a flesh-bond story in which the villain is a Jew who prefers his ducats to his daughter, and a pound of flesh to his ducats, and his living to his religion. To say of someone that he wants his pound of flesh is still to say that he wants not justice but vengeance.

Lastly, however central Shylock has become, Shakespeare interwove the flesh-bond story with the casket story and brought Portia to the rescue. She acts as a kind of providence in his play, preaching a mercy which she later extends to her husband. At the trial's climax she asks a leading question: 'What mercy can you render him, Antonio?' Shakespeare's audience are thus invited to see Antonio's sentence as Christian mercy, exchanging kindness for Shylock's cruelty. What weight should such a strong historical probability have with us? We may think it unfair that Shylock has to become a Christian or die. But we are dealing with Shakespeare's play rather than another play which we might prefer. It belongs then, but it also lives now. It pleases us, but it can still trouble us.

# PART SEVEN

# BROADER PERSPECTIVES

## FURTHER READING

### EDITIONS OF *THE MERCHANT OF VENICE*

Below are the most common modern editions.

**John Russell Brown, ed., The Arden Shakespeare, Methuen. 1955, revised 1961**

Good full academic edition, with reliable glosses and notes; though now a little old it is fuller than Mahood or Halio

**J.L. Halio, ed., The Oxford Shakespeare, Clarendon Press, 1993; World Classics, Oxford University Press, 1994**

Excellent. Full academic edition, with reliable glosses and notes

**G.B. Harrison, ed., Penguin Shakespeare, Penguin Popular Classics, 1955**

A school edition, originally published in the 1930s; in its Popular Classic form it has no introduction or notes and is not ideal for examinees

**Bernard Lott, ed., New Swan Shakespeare, Longman, 1962, 1964**

A school edition with good notes, except on matters which might bring a blush to the cheek of the young person

**M.M. Mahood, ed., New Cambridge Shakespeare, Cambridge University Press, 1987**

Mahood is a literary critic as well as a scholar. A good full academic edition. This is the text which has been used to accompany this Note

**W. Moelwyn Merchant, ed., The New Penguin Shakespeare, Penguin, 1967**

Better than Harrison. Some notes. Eccentric introduction

**Kenneth Myrick, ed., The Signet Shakespeare, Signet, 1965**

A good college edition

**J.H. Walter, ed., The Players' Shakespeare, Heinemann, 1960**

A school edition which silently omits text which might be considered *risqué*

SINGLE-VOLUME COLLECTED EDITIONS

Peter Alexander, ed., *William Shakespeare: the Complete Works*, Collins, 1951

Convenient: good brief introductions, simple glossary, but no notes

Stanley Wells and Gary Taylor, gen. eds, *Works*, Oxford University Press, 1986 (known as the Oxford Shakespeare)

The version sold as the Compact Edition of the Oxford Shakespeare is convenient, and has good introductions, simple glossary, but no notes. However, a radical editorial policy has changed familiar texts in ways that some scholars dislike or dispute. But the Oxford Shakespeare is already influential

CRITICAL WORKS

C. L. Barber, *Shakespeare's Festive Comedy*, 2nd edn, Oxford University Press, 1972

A good general study of the comedies

J.C. Bulman, *Text in Performance: The Merchant of Venice*, Manchester University Press, 1991

Theatre history

John Gross, *Shylock: Four Hundred Years in the Life of a Legend*, Vintage, 1994

A wide-ranging survey

John Lyon, *The Merchant of Venice*, Harvester, 1988

A sophisticated introduction which pays attention to recent criticism

Murray Roston, *Sixteenth-Century English Literature*, Macmillan, 1982

A sound general introduction, with a good sketch of Shakespeare's literary career

John Wilders, ed., *'The Merchant of Venice': A Casebook*, Macmillan, 1962

A selection of critical articles

| World events | Shakespeare's life | Literature / drama |
|---|---|---|
| **1290** Jews expelled from England by Edward I | | **Late 13th c** (c.) *Gesta Romanorum* (source) |
| **1295** Marco Polo returns to Venice after travels in China | | |
| **1380** Venice's 100-year feud with Genoa ends | | |
| **1400-90** (c.) Venice at height of maritime power | | |
| **1492** Columbus sets sails for America | | |
| **1490s** Venice's power at sea in decline | | |
| | | **1513** Niccolò Machiavelli, *The Prince* |
| **1516** Jews in Venice confined to Ghetto | | |
| | | **1528** Castiglione's *Book of the Courtier* |
| **1534** Henry VIII breaks with Rome | | |
| **1556** Archbishop Cranmer burnt at stake | | |
| **1558** Elizabeth I accedes to throne | | **1558** Trans. of Ser Giovanni of Florence, *Il Pecorone* (late 14th-c. source) |
| | | **1562** Lope de Vega, Spanish dramatist, born |
| | **1564** (26 April) **William Shakespeare** baptised, Stratford-upon-Avon | |
| **1566** Royal Exchange founded | | |
| **1570** Elizabeth I excommunicated by Pope Pius V | | |
| **1572** Death of Venetian painter Titian | | |
| | **1576** James Burbage builds the first theatre in England, at Shoreditch | |
| **1577** Francis Drake sets out on voyage round the world | | |
| | | **1578** (c.) *The Jew* (lost play -? source) |
| | | **1580** (c.) Sir Philip Sidney, *An Apologie for Poetrie;* Anthony Munday, *Zelauto* (source) |
| | **1582** Shakespeare marries Anne Hathaway | |
| | **1583** Their daughter, Susanna, is born | |
| **1584** Raleigh's sailors land in Virginia | | |
| | **1585** Their twins, Hamnet and Judith, born | |
| **1587** Execution of Mary Queen of Scots | | |
| **1588** The Spanish Armada defeated | | **1588-9** Thomas Kyd, *The Spanish Tragedy* |
| | | **1589** Christopher Marlowe, *The Jew of Malta* (source) |
| | | **1590** Edmund Spenser, *Faerie Queene* (Books I-III) |

| World events | Shakespeare's life | Literature / drama |
|---|---|---|
| | late **1580s - early 90s** Probably writes *Henry VI (Parts I, II, III)* and *Richard III* | |
| **1592** Rialto Bridge completed. Plague in London closes theatres | **1592** Recorded as being a London actor and an 'upstart crow' | |
| | **1592-4** Writes *Comedy of Errors* | |
| | **1594** onwards Writes exclusively for the Lord Chamberlain's Men | |
| | **1595** (pre-) *Two Gentlemen of Verona, The Taming of the Shrew* and *Love's Labour's Lost* probably written | |
| | **1595** (c.) *Romeo and Juliet* | |
| **1596** English raid on Cadiz | **1596-8** First performance, **The Merchant of Venice** | **1596** English trans. of Alexandre Silvain, *The Orator* (source) |
| | **1598/9** Globe Theatre built at Southwark | |
| | **1600** *A Midsummer Night's Dream, Much Ado about Nothing* and **The Merchant of Venice** printed in quartos | |
| | **1600-1** *Hamlet* | |
| | **1600-2** *Twelfth Night* written | |
| **1603** Death of Queen Elizabeth Tudor; accession of James Stuart | **1603** onwards His company enjoys patronage of James I as the King's Men | |
| | **1604** *Othello* performed | |
| **1605** Discovery of Guy Fawkes's plot | **1605** First version of *King Lear* | **1605** Cervantes, *Don Quijote de la Mancha* |
| | **1606** *Macbeth* | |
| | **1606-7** *Antony and Cleopatra* | |
| | **1608** The King's Men acquire Blackfriars Theatre for winter performances | |
| **1610** William Harvey discovers circulation of blood | | |
| | **1611** *Cymboline, The Winter's Tale* and *The Tempest* performed | |
| **1612** Last burning of heretics in England | | |
| | **1613** Globe Theatre burns down | |
| | **1616** Death of William Shakespeare | |
| **1618** Raleigh executed for treason Thirty Years War begins in Europe | | |
| | | **1622** Birth of French dramatist Molière |
| | **1623** First folio of Shakespeare's works | |
| **1655** Under Cromwell. Jews formally readmitted to England | | |

**allegory** the sustained suggestion of deeper, usually moral, meaning in a story

**aside** a stage direction indicating the convention that the following speech is supposed to be inaudible to other characters onstage; like a soliloquy, it serves to communicate private thoughts

**comedic** characteristic of comedy and of the conventions of comedy, when a confusion of identities is resolved in a happy ending; as distinct from **comic,** laughable

**couplet** a pair of rhyming lines

**decorum** rhetorical principle that style must match topic, and that there is a hierarchy of suitable styles: high for tragedy, low for farce, and so forth

**exposition** the giving of information essential to the story

**irony** saying one thing while meaning another; using words to convey the opposite of their literal meaning; saying something that has one meaning for someone knowledgeable about a situation and another meaning for those who are not; incongruity between what might be expected and what actually happens; ill-timed arrival of an event which had been hoped for

**malapropism** using the wrong word; from French *mal à propos*; after Mrs Malaprop (Mrs Mistake) in Sheridan's *The Rivals*, 1755

**mock-heroic** using heroic comparisons for playful purposes

**paradox** a statement that seems self-contradictory, absurd or unbelievable, yet which contains a truth

**parody** imitation of the style of a well-known work, exaggerating its features for comic purposes

**register** linguistic term for the level of the vocabulary from which words are taken, see decorum

**romance** a story of marvellous adventure, with elements of folk- and fairytale, in which wishes are fulfilled: the right casket is chosen; long-lost relatives are reunited; Jack shall have Jill and all shall be well. Often combined with comedy; not necessarily a love story, in the modern sense of the word 'romantic'

**stage business** physical actions accompanying or clarifying the words of the actors

# AUTHORS OF THIS NOTE

Michael Alexander is Berry Professor of English Literature in the University of St Andrews, Scotland. He is author of verse translations of *Beowulf* and of *The Earliest English Poems* in Penguin Classics, and has edited *The Canterbury Tales: The First Fragment* for Penguin. He has written on modern as well as medieval poetry, and is currently writing a History of English Literature for Macmillan.

Mary Alexander has a degree in English from the University of Melbourne and Diplomas in Education from La Trobe University and the Institute of Education, London University. She has taught English in schools in Australia and Britain, and currently teaches A-Level English Literature at St Leonards School in St Andrews, Scotland.

# Notes

# NOTES

# NOTES

# NOTES

# NOTES

# NOTES

# NOTES

# NOTES

# NOTES

## York Notes Advanced (£3.99 each)

Margaret Atwood
*The Handmaid's Tale*

Jane Austen
*Emma*

Jane Austen
*Pride and Prejudice*

William Blake
*Songs of Innocence and of Experience*

Charlotte Brontë
*Jane Eyre*

Emily Brontë
*Wuthering Heights*

Geoffrey Chaucer
*The Wife of Bath's Prologue and Tale*

Joseph Conrad
*Heart of Darkness*

Charles Dickens
*Great Expectations*

F. Scott Fitzgerald
*The Great Gatsby*

Thomas Hardy
*Tess of the d'Urbervilles*

Seamus Heaney
*Selected Poems*

James Joyce
*Dubliners*

Arthur Miller
*Death of a Salesman*

William Shakespeare
*Antony and Cleopatra*

William Shakespeare
*Hamlet*

William Shakespeare
*King Lear*

William Shakespeare
*The Merchant of Venice*

William Shakespeare
*Much Ado About Nothing*

William Shakespeare
*Othello*

William Shakespeare
*Romeo and Juliet*

William Shakespeare
*The Tempest*

Mary Shelley
*Frankenstein*

Alice Walker
*The Color Purple*

Tennessee Williams
*A Streetcar Named Desire*

John Webster
*The Duchess of Malfi*

## GCSE and equivalent levels (£3.50 each)

| | |
|---|---|
| Harold Brighouse<br>*Hobson's Choice* | J.B. Priestley<br>*An Inspector Calls* |
| Charles Dickens<br>*Great Expectations* | J.D. Salinger<br>*The Catcher in the Rye* |
| Charles Dickens<br>*Hard Times* | William Shakespeare<br>*Macbeth* |
| George Eliot<br>*Silas Marner* | William Shakespeare<br>*The Merchant of Venice* |
| William Golding<br>*Lord of the Flies* | William Shakespeare<br>*Romeo and Juliet* |
| Thomas Hardy<br>*The Mayor of Casterbridge* | William Shakespeare<br>*Twelfth Night* |
| Susan Hill<br>*I'm the King of the Castle* | George Bernard Shaw<br>*Pygmalion* |
| Barry Hines<br>*A Kestrel for a Knave* | John Steinbeck<br>*Of Mice and Men* |
| Harper Lee<br>*To Kill a Mockingbird* | Mildred D. Taylor<br>*Roll of Thunder, Hear My Cry* |
| Arthur Miller<br>*A View from the Bridge* | James Watson<br>*Talking in Whispers* |
| Arthur Miller<br>*The Crucible* | *A Choice of Poets* |
| George Orwell<br>*Animal Farm* | *Nineteenth Century Short Stories*<br><br>*Poetry of the First World War* |

Chinua Achebe
*Things Fall Apart*

Edward Albee
*Who's Afraid of Virginia Woolf?*

Maya Angelou
*I Know Why The Caged Bird Sings*

Jane Austen
*Mansfield Park*

Jane Austen
*Northanger Abbey*

Jane Austen
*Persuasion*

Jane Austen
*Pride and Prejudice*

Jane Austen
*Sense and Sensibility*

Samuel Beckett
*Waiting for Godot*

John Betjeman
*Selected Poems*

Robert Bolt
*A Man for All Seasons*

Charlotte Brontë
*Jane Eyre*

Emily Brontë
*Wuthering Heights*

Robert Burns
*Selected Poems*

Lord Byron
*Selected Poems*

Geoffrey Chaucer
*The Franklin's Tale*

Geoffrey Chaucer
*The Knight's Tale*

Geoffrey Chaucer
*The Merchant's Tale*

Geoffrey Chaucer
*The Miller's Tale*

Geoffrey Chaucer
*The Nun's Priest's Tale*

Geoffrey Chaucer
*The Pardoner's Tale*

Geoffrey Chaucer
*Prologue to the Canterbury Tales*

Samuel Taylor Coleridge
*Selected Poems*

Daniel Defoe
*Moll Flanders*

Daniel Defoe
*Robinson Crusoe*

Shelagh Delaney
*A Taste of Honey*

Charles Dickens
*Bleak House*

Charles Dickens
*David Copperfield*

Charles Dickens
*Oliver Twist*

Emily Dickinson
*Selected Poems*

John Donne
*Selected Poems*

Douglas Dunn
*Selected Poems*

George Eliot
*Middlemarch*

George Eliot
*The Mill on the Floss*

T.S. Eliot
*The Waste Land*

T.S. Eliot
*Selected Poems*

Henry Fielding
*Joseph Andrews*

E.M. Forster
*Howards End*

E.M. Forster
*A Passage to India*

John Fowles
*The French Lieutenant's Woman*

Elizabeth Gaskell
*North and South*

Oliver Goldsmith
*She Stoops to Conquer*

Graham Greene
*Brighton Rock*

Graham Greene
*The Heart of the Matter*

Graham Greene
*The Power and the Glory*

Willis Hall
*The Long and the Short and the Tall*

Thomas Hardy
*Far from the Madding Crowd*

Thomas Hardy
*Jude the Obscure*

Thomas Hardy
*The Return of the Native*

Thomas Hardy
*Selected Poems*

Thomas Hardy
*Tess of the d'Urbervilles*

L.P. Hartley
*The Go-Between*

Nathaniel Hawthorne
*The Scarlet Letter*

Seamus Heaney
*Selected Poems*

Ernest Hemingway
*A Farewell to Arms*

Ernest Hemingway
*The Old Man and the Sea*

Homer
*The Iliad*

Homer
*The Odyssey*

Gerard Manley Hopkins
*Selected Poems*

Ted Hughes
*Selected Poems*

Aldous Huxley
*Brave New World*

Henry James
*Portrait of a Lady*

Ben Jonson
*The Alchemist*

Ben Jonson
*Volpone*

James Joyce
*A Portrait of the Artist as a Young Man*

John Keats
*Selected Poems*

Philip Larkin
*Selected Poems*

D.H. Lawrence
*The Rainbow*

D.H. Lawrence
*Selected Stories*

D.H. Lawrence
*Sons and Lovers*

D.H. Lawrence
*Women in Love*

Louise Lawrence
*Children of the Dust*

Laurie Lee
*Cider with Rosie*

Christopher Marlowe
*Doctor Faustus*

John Milton
*Paradise Lost Bks I & II*

John Milton
*Paradise Lost IV & IX*

Robert O'Brien
*Z for Zachariah*

Sean O'Casey
*Juno and the Paycock*

George Orwell
*Nineteen Eighty-four*

John Osborne
*Look Back in Anger*

Wilfred Owen
*Selected Poems*

Harold Pinter
*The Caretaker*

Sylvia Plath
*Selected Works*

Alexander Pope
*Selected Poems*

Jean Rhys
*Wide Sargasso Sea*

Willy Russell
*Educating Rita*

Willy Russell
*Our Day Out*

William Shakespeare
*As You Like It*

William Shakespeare
*Coriolanus*

William Shakespeare
*Henry IV Pt 1*

William Shakespeare
*Henry IV Pt II*

William Shakespeare
*Henry V*

William Shakespeare
*Julius Caesar*

William Shakespeare
*Measure for Measure*

William Shakespeare
*A Midsummer Night's Dream*

William Shakespeare
*Richard II*

William Shakespeare
*Richard III*

William Shakespeare
*Sonnets*

William Shakespeare
*The Taming of the Shrew*

William Shakespeare
*The Tempest*

William Shakespeare
*The Winter's Tale*

George Bernard Shaw
*Arms and the Man*

George Bernard Shaw
*Saint Joan*

Richard Brinsley Sheridan
*The Rivals*

R.C. Sherriff
*Journey's End*

Rukshana Smith
*Salt on the Snow*

Muriel Spark
*The Prime of Miss Jean Brodie*

John Steinbeck
*The Grapes of Wrath*

John Steinbeck
*The Pearl*

R.L. Stevenson
*Dr Jekyll and Mr Hyde*

Tom Stoppard
*Rosencrantz and Guildenstern are Dead*

Jonathan Swift
*Gulliver's Travels*

Robert Swindells
*Daz 4 Zoe*

John Millington Synge
*The Playboy of the Western World*

W.M. Thackeray
*Vanity Fair*

Mark Twain
*Huckleberry Finn*

Virgil
*The Aeneid*

Derek Walcott
*Selected Poems*

Oscar Wilde
*The Importance of Being Earnest*

Tennessee Williams
*Cat on a Hot Tin Roof*

Tennessee Williams
*The Glass Menagerie*

Virginia Woolf
*Mrs Dalloway*

Virginia Woolf
*To the Lighthouse*

William Wordsworth
*Selected Poems*

W.B. Yeats
*Selected Poems*

*Six Women Poets*

# York Notes – the Ultimate Literature Guides

York Notes are recognised as the best literature study guides.
If you have enjoyed using this book and have found it useful, you
can now order others directly from us – simply follow the ordering
instructions below.

## HOW TO ORDER

Decide which title(s) you require and then order in one of the following
ways:

### Booksellers
All titles available from good bookstores.

### By post
List the title(s) you require in the space provided overleaf,
select your method of payment, complete your name and
address details and return your completed order form and
payment to:

> *Addison Wesley Longman Ltd*
> *PO BOX 88*
> *Harlow*
> *Essex CM19 5SR*

### By phone
Call our Customer Information Centre on 01279 623923 to
place your order, quoting mail number: HEYN1.

### By fax
Complete the order form overleaf, ensuring you fill in your
name and address details and method of payment, and fax it
to us on 01279 414130.

### By e-mail
E-mail your order to us on awlhe.orders@awl.co.uk listing
title(s) and quantity required and providing full name and
address details as requested overleaf. Please quote mail
number: HEYN1. Please do not send credit card details by
e-mail.

# York Notes Order Form

## Titles required:

| Quantity | Title/ISBN | Price |
|---|---|---|
| | | |
| | | |
| | | |
| | | |
| | | |
| | | |

Sub total _____
Please add £2.50 postage & packing _____
*(P & P is free for orders over £50)* _____
**Total** _____

Mail no: HEYN1

Your Name _____
Your Address _____
_____

Postcode _____ Telephone _____

## Method of payment

☐ I enclose a cheque or a P/O for £_____ made payable to
Addison Wesley Longman Ltd

☐ Please charge my Visa/Access/AMEX/Diners Club card
Number _____ Expiry Date _____
Signature _____ Date _____

*(please ensure that the address given above is the same as for your credit card)*

*Prices and other details are correct at time of going to press but may change without notice. All orders are subject to status.*

☐ *Please tick this box if you would like a complete listing of Longman Study Guides (suitable for GCSE and A-level students)*

York Press

Longman

Addison
Wesley
Longman